MW01611205

Driven by Destiny

Life Lessons From
Formula 1 Legends

E.J. Agosti

To Mops and Dizz for a lifetime of love and support, and F1 simulations.

To Jessica and James for always being you and for Go-Karting with me.

You are my everything xxxx

Table of Contents

Acknowledgement

Driver Illustrations by Lauren Ketchell, U.K.

Thank you, Lauren, for your dedication to this project.

Prologue:

The Formation Lap

The roar of the engines. The smell of burning rubber. The thrill of seeing a speeding machine whizzing by at a breathtaking speed. These are the moments that captured my imagination, drawing me into a world where heroes are made, dreams are shattered, and every second counts. The intensity of a Formula 1 race is unlike anything else. The anticipation as the lights go out, the deafening noise of 20 cars tearing down the straight, and the precision of each maneuver—all create a unique atmosphere of tension, emotion, and adrenaline.

It's this edge of danger that fuels the adrenaline rush. As cars speed through tight corners at hundreds of miles per hour, the drivers walk a fine line between control and chaos. The smallest mistake can have catastrophic consequences, yet it's this very risk that makes the sport so exhilarating. The sensation of being so close to death, of knowing that every decision could be your last, is a stark reminder of what it means to be truly alive. It's in these high-pressure moments when a person's character is revealed and legends are born.

I became fascinated by the drivers—their dedication, their struggles, and the virtues they embody. It wasn't just about the races they won or the records they broke. It was about their journeys, the setbacks they faced, and the way they pushed through when it seemed impossible. Each driver has a unique story, but all of them share a common thread: the ability to turn adversity into strength.

Take Juan Manuel Fangio, for example. He wasn't just a five-time world champion—he was a symbol of resilience. Fangio's career spanned a challenging era, marked by fierce competition and personal loss. Yet he kept going, bouncing back from injuries and setbacks. His story taught me that resilience is more than just surviving hardship—it's about using those hardships to fuel your determination and keep moving forward.

Or consider Ayrton Senna, whose determination on the track was unmatched. His focus, intensity, and drive made him a legend. But it wasn't just his skill behind the wheel that inspired me—it was his passion for the sport and his commitment to making it safer for everyone. Senna's tragic death in 1994 was a turning point for Formula 1, leading to significant safety changes. His legacy is a powerful reminder that one person's determination can bring about meaningful change.

Bruce McLaren's commitment to innovation and teamwork was another source of inspiration. Despite facing his own set of challenges, McLaren built a team that has become a staple in Formula 1 history. His anecdote reveals the power of collaboration and how bringing together the right people can lead to remarkable achievements.

Michael Schumacher, the seven-time world champion, showcased unparalleled leadership and dominance. His success at Ferrari in the early 2000s was a testament to his skill and determination. Schumacher's ability to rally his team and push them to new heights was a masterclass in leadership and strategic thinking.

Fernando Alonso's journey is a story of humbleness and continuous improvement. Despite being a two-time world champion, Alonso's career has been marked by ups and downs. Yet, his unwavering commitment to the sport and his humility in the face of adversity have made him a respected figure in the Formula 1 community.

Lewis Hamilton's perseverance in the face of adversity is legendary. As the first Black driver to win a Formula 1 championship, Hamilton faced unique challenges. Yet, he persevered, breaking records and using his platform to advocate for diversity and inclusion within the sport. His journey is a testament to the power of perseverance and the impact it can have on the world.

Even the team principals, like Toto Wolff, played a role in shaping my perspective. His strategic approach to team management and willingness to take risks, even when they didn't always pay off, demonstrated the importance of boldness in pursuit of success. Wolff's gamble with the 2022 W13 vehicle—a risk that ultimately didn't work out—reminded me that success in any field involves both risk and uncertainty.

Carlos Sainz Jr., known for his consistent dedication to his team, shows that loyalty is not just about sticking around—it's about putting in the work, even when things are tough. His career is a testament to the value of perseverance and commitment, whether you're in the spotlight or working quietly behind the scenes. His approach to the sport taught me the significance of standing by your values and supporting those who believe in you. His journey inspired me to understand that loyalty is a driving force that can push you further than you'd imagine.

On the other hand, Max Verstappen's disciplined approach to racing demonstrates how a structured mindset can lead to success. Despite his young age, Verstappen's rigorous focus on his goals and his relentless pursuit of excellence are traits that any aspiring person can learn from. He showed me that discipline isn't about rigid routines—it's about cultivating a mindset that allows you to adapt and improve continuously. His complex relationship with his father, who has been both a mentor and a challenging presence, underlines the significance of learning from every experience and capitalizing on it to grow stronger.

Through these stories, I found inspiration and guidance for my journey. I saw how these characters navigated challenges, overcame obstacles, and became icons in the world of Formula 1. I wanted to share these stories because I believe they hold valuable lessons for anyone striving to achieve their goals. Whether you're pursuing a career, chasing a dream, or simply trying to be the best version of yourself, there's something to learn from these remarkable individuals.

So, join me as we explore the high-speed world of Formula 1 through the lens of its most iconic characters. Together, we'll uncover the virtues and life lessons that have driven these individuals to greatness. As you read their stories, I hope you'll find inspiration, motivation, and perhaps even a few new insights to carry with you on your own journey.

Let's dive in and see what we can learn from the legends of the most prestigious motorsport in the world.

Chapter 1:

Juan Manuel Fangio—

Resilience

Resilience. It's a word that holds deep meaning, especially when you've faced a challenge that seemed insurmountable. I remember a moment in my life when I felt like everything was falling apart when the path ahead seemed uncertain and fraught with obstacles.

It was during this time that I learned the true value of resilience, the quiet yet powerful strength that keeps you moving forward, even when every instinct tells you to give up. This personal journey of mine was filled with setbacks and disappointment, yet it was also where I discovered an inner resolve I never knew I had.

As I reflect on that period of my life, I can't help but think of the world of Formula 1. It's a realm where resilience isn't just a personal trait—it's a critical survival skill. The intense speed, the unrelenting competition, the risks—every moment on the track is a test of temperament and endurance. Drivers must be constantly on edge and fully aware that one wrong move could spell disaster. Yet, during this high-octane environment, certain figures stand out for their unwavering resilience and their ability to face adversity head-on and come out on top.

Juan Manuel Fangio is one such figure. Known as "El Chueco," the Argentine entered Formula 1 from a background that many in Europe might have dismissed. As a South American driver, Fangio had to contend with stereotypes and preconceived notions about his skill and capability, not to mention the abysmal economic disadvantage. Despite his undeniable talent, he was often viewed with skepticism, as if his background made him less worthy of success. Yet "El Chueco" had something that couldn't be denied: an indomitable spirit and a relentless drive to prove himself.

In the world of motorsport, where precision and speed are everything, Fangio's journey was anything but straightforward. His road to success was paved with hardships and challenges, yet he never wavered. He faced the intense competition, the pressure, and the constant danger with a calm demeanor and a fierce determination. His resilience became a hallmark of his career, leading him to become one of the most successful drivers in Formula 1 history.

His story is a testament to the power of resilience, to the idea that no matter where you come from or what you face, you can achieve greatness if you refuse to give up. His journey serves as a source of inspiration for anyone who's ever felt underestimated or out of place, proving that resilience can turn the impossible into reality.

From Rags to Racetracks

From the bosom of a family of Italian immigrants, a legend was born in the Buenos Aires area of Balcarce on June 24, 1911. Juan Manuel was the fourth child of Loreto Fangio and Herminia Déramo. The young Italian couple met in Argentina after their families moved to the global south to escape the instability and incipient war that loomed over the old continent at the beginning of that century.

Loreto worked in construction. With a confident but strict personality, he taught his children the trades of the time to ensure their future (Museo Juan Manuel Fangio, n.d.).

Juan Manuel did not want to be a bricklayer but he helped his father in his free time outside of school. Loreto, who saw in his son great talent and skill with his hands, decided to take little Juan Manuel, then 9 years old, to work in his friend Francisco's blacksmith shop, where the area's carriages were serviced and all kinds of crafts and metal forging were made.

At 10 years old, Juan Manuel Fangio attended the afternoon shift at the Balcarce school and dedicated his mornings to working in the workshop. He made sure to arrive early every morning to move a chain-drive Panhard Levassor. He would stand on the starter handle and start it. Then he would back up to clean the floor and return it to its place. He would repeat the operation several times entertained by the rudiments of driving a car—the first he had ever had in his hands.

The spark of "El Chueco" was lit. The boy from the Buenos Aires suburbs had his first contact with his destiny.

A year later, he started working at the car dealership of Don Carlini, a car dealer in the area. With him, he learned to drive correctly because Carlini would ask him to drive his truck when he went hunting. They would also go around the area repairing agricultural machinery and sometimes he would allow Juan Manuel to drive.

Hungry for knowledge, young Juan Manuel left behind his first mentor to accept the offer of a Ford mechanic, who invited him to work and learn with him in the local workshop.

Mechanic Guillermo Spain guided him through the parts of the engine. At the age of 13, Juan Manuel began working as a mechanic's assistant in the workshop of Miguel Viggiano, a renowned local pilot.

The year was 1927, and young Fangio became a skilled mechanic. Fate knocks on his door once again. This time, as part of his salary, he received a four-cylinder Overland car. "El Chueco" is thirsting for speed (TN Deportivo, 2022).

He reconditioned the car to prepare it for the tracks. But his debut took another two years to arrive. He fell ill with pleurisy at the age of 16 and had to rest for almost a full year.

Before setting out to make his name on the track, Juan Manuel Fangio tried out other sports as well. He played soccer for the Rivadavia Club, standing out for his agility and reflexes.

In 1929, as he enjoyed optimal health, young Fangio met Manuel Ayerza, a local driver in the workshop and helped him prepare his 1928 Chevrolet for the next race. Ayerza saw in him a unique talent and eloquence and invited him to escort him in the race—this was the debut of the Argentine star in the world of motorsports.

The year was 1932, and at 21 years old, Juan Manuel dreamed big. He wanted to run around the world. But it seemed impossible to leave that dusty and gray Balcarce. That's when the idea of setting up a workshop with his friend José Duffard arose. In those days, they had some clients and would fix their cars at their house. Don Loreto offered him a piece of land next to his house, and they built a workshop there. Some old car chassis beams were used as beams in the workshop; zinc sheets, they would "get" at night from an abandoned house in the countryside, were used to build the roof. A friend who did carpentry, along with Juan Manuel and José Duffard, dug the pit for the dirt floor workshop. Others raised 80 pesos to buy tools. A football friend, Francisco Cavallotti, joined the workshop and contributed an old truck as capital.

On October 25, 1936, his fate was sealed: Fangio debuted as a driver under the pseudonym "Rivadavia" in a blue 1929 Ford Model A No. 19, which operated as a taxi and was owned by the father of a friend of his. They had to abandon the race while they were third with two laps to go because of a technical fault—the Ford was more of a workhorse than a battle horse.

The years went by and the "El Chueco" workshop grew. He also made it his career as a driver. He was well known on the local circuit for his cunning and bravery on the track, but he always ended up disqualified or not completing the laps for technical reasons. He needed a good car that allowed him to show what he was made of. But in a world harassed by war and Argentina in full industrial development, there were not enough resources.

It was already 1940. Juan Manuel was 29 years old. Sometimes, he walked through his workshop and would see a bolt on the floor. He would kick it and pretend that he was the champion of the Argentine Soccer League and wore a Rivadavia shirt. Was he already too old to be a champion at anything? Was that fate reserved only for the children of ranchers who wore white shirts and owned the expensive cars that his oiled hands repaired? One of these times, he looked down and saw some damaged cars that needed his attention. And in that moment, he was certain: He would be a world motorsports champion.

In October of that year, he got a unique opportunity: To race on the most important motorsport circuit in South America, the Gran Turismo Carretera.

After 9,500 km of competition through Argentina, Bolivia, and Peru, he won his first race. It was the International Grand Prix of the North, Buenos Aires-Lima-Buenos Aires, in which he raced accompanied by his friend H. Tieri in a green 1940 Chevrolet showing a white number 26. Thus, that year he became the Argentine Champion of Road Tourism.

The following year, he defended and renewed his title and achieved his first victory abroad: defeating the Ford ambassador Oscar Gálvez on Brazilian soil (TN Deportivo, 2022).

The rocket that carried within it the promise of becoming a world motorsport champion from a remote suburban neighborhood on the shores of the Río de la Plata was about to take off. But then, everything froze.

War was ravaging the world and neither Juan Manuel nor anyone else knew what was going to happen. Once again, the young Chueco's desires seemed to fade into the thin air.

It was not until 1946, as the dust of war settled, that mechanical activity resumed in the global south and Juan Manuel returned to the tracks.

The young Chueco dreamed again of running in a World Cup and becoming Champion.

Triumphs and Trials

All eyes were on him: the promise. Race by race, he demonstrated his dominance on the tracks and his immense humility off them.

It was the year 1948 when the French team Naphtha Course placed its faith in the young Juan Manuel and entrusted him with a Maserati 4CL 1500 to race the Palermo circuit. With the same hands that swept the floor of his father's workshop, he now drove a true Grand Prix machine.

That year was the first of many full of victories and cheers for the kid from Balcarce, whose name was beginning to resonate among European ears.

In July, he left on a study trip to the United States and Europe, visiting factories and circuits with other drivers and directors of the Argentine Automobile Club.

In France, Amadeo Gordini invited him to compete with a Simca-Gordini in Reims. It was his debut in Grand Prix races in Europe, and although his performance was not as excellent as usual, it was good enough to attract the attention of the owners of some of the most important teams in the world.

Moved more by the dream of the boy from Balcarce than by the ambition of the pilot, Juan Manuel moved to Italy along with his team, the "Aquiles Varzi." During that season, he participated in 10 races and won 6 of them. When he returned to his native country, he received cheers and mentions of all kinds (Museo Juan Manuel Fangio, n.d.).

It was 1950, and he had the opportunity to sign a contract with Alfa Romeo after he tested one of his cars in a race where he became champion. Defending the honor of this team, the kid from Balcarce competed in his first world championship in Formula 1.

That first World Cup presented him with a harsh reality. He didn't get points and wore out the car in qualifying. His European teammates and rivals seemed to master more techniques and resolve situations better than him as well. His mechanical equipment was as good as theirs and his car had nothing to envy the other competing teams for. But for some reason, Juan Manuel stagnated.

Sometimes, "El Chueco" even thought that perhaps the Italian pilots who made fun of him by calling him the "false Italian" or the "sudaca" were not wrong about his abilities. Maybe he was the best in Argentina but he couldn't compare to the world's elite.

Those who knew him say that Fangio was a quiet, humble guy, with an agile and insightful humor. He did not drink or smoke and despite his reputation and good looks, he was rather shy with women. They say that what he had to say, he said on the track, without speaking a word. He was a facts guy.

The facts spoke for him in 1951. He began his second season for the World Championship in an Alfa Romeo 159 and triumphed in the Swiss GP in Berne on May 27, the European GP in Reims on July 1, and the Spanish GP at the Pedralbes Circuit in Barcelona on October 28. There, he conquered his first Drivers' Championship, his first World Champion title.

It was February 1952. Mercedes-Benz recognized his talent and appointed him a dealer of the brand. This was an honor reserved only for those who represented the values of excellence and performance that the iconic German brand sought. This recognition of his mastery and dedication reflected his growing popularity and respect in the world of motorsports.

In his native Argentina, Fangio continued his winning streak. On March 9, he won the President Perón Award, and a week later, on March 16, the Eva Perón Award. These victories reaffirmed him as a national hero, a figure who inspired many with his bravery and skill. Fangio was not only an exceptional driver but also a symbol of pride for his country.

Success crossed the borders to Uruguay, where on March 23 and 30, Fangio won victories at the Piriápolis Circuit. These races, all in a Ferrari 125, demonstrated his adaptability and ability to win in different conditions and against a variety of opponents.

On June 7, Fangio competed in Ireland in a BRM, but his itinerary took him to Italy for a competition at Monza on June 8, this time in a Maserati. The journey was exhausting, much of which he did alone in a car, arriving just hours before the race. During the third turn, in the dangerous Lesmo corner, Fangio suffered a serious accident. The impact was so severe that it left him hospitalized for almost four months—a period of uncertainty and pain for him and his fans (Museo Juan Manuel Fangio, n.d.).

The world of motorsport seemed to move forward without him, and harsh comments were made that suggested his moment of glory had passed. However, Fangio was a man of unwavering determination, and his heart burned with the desire to return to the top.

In early 1954, Fangio began his recovery by racing a Maserati 250F and achieving solid results. On January 17, he won the Grand Prix of the Argentine Republic and demonstrated that his skill had not diminished despite the time of inactivity. Then, on June 20, he won the Belgian Grand Prix at the iconic Spa-

Francorchamps circuit. These victories were not only a testament to his innate talent but also served to reaffirm his place in the sport.

That same year, Fangio signed a contract with Mercedes-Benz, a move that would change the course of his career and that of motorsports. With the powerful "Silver Arrow" W196, the Argentine driver began to score points in the World Championship. His debut with Mercedes-Benz was impressive and he won the French Grand Prix at Reims on July 4. The forcefulness of that victory was a message to all those who doubted his return.

But the kid from Balcarce longed for more glory. On August 1, he won the European Grand Prix at the Nürburgring, one of the most challenging circuits in the world. He continued his winning streak at the Swiss Grand Prix in Bern on August 22 and at the Italian Grand Prix in Monza on September 5. These successive victories showed his dominance once again.

With these impressive performances, Fangio won his second World Drivers' Championship. This achievement, only three years after an accident that many thought would keep him permanently off the track, demonstrated the resilience and competitive spirit of the Argentine driver.

As the championship progressed, Fangio continued to show his skill and talent. On July 14, he won the British Grand Prix at the Silverstone circuit, one of the most iconic circuits in motorsport. The victory was overwhelming and solidified his position as one of the favorites for the world title.

On August 5, the Argentine driver competed in the German Grand Prix at the Nürburgring, a circuit famous for its difficulty and technical demands. It was on this track that Fangio demonstrated his experience and skill and achieved another victory with the Lancia-Ferrari D50. With this victory, he strengthened his position in the world championship standings.

The climax came on September 2, at the Italian Grand Prix at the Monza circuit. Fangio not only had to run a flawless race, but he also needed some strategy to secure his fourth world title. In a show of camaraderie and generosity, British driver Peter Collins, Fangio's teammate, gave him his car after "El Chueco" suffered mechanical problems. With this gesture, Fangio was able to qualify second, which allowed him to add the necessary points to win his fourth World Drivers' Championship.

This act of camaraderie and Fangio's final triumph demonstrated that motorsport is more than just competition and rivalry—it is also teamwork and mutual respect. Fangio's fourth world title with Ferrari solidified his place as one of the greatest drivers of all time, and his ability to adapt and succeed, even in the face of adversity, made him a living legend.

In 1957, Juan Manuel Fangio signed a contract with Maserati to race the 250F model, and his dominance in Formula 1 continued firmly. He won four F1 World Championship qualifying races, starting with the Argentine Grand Prix on January 13. Fangio showed his mastery at every circuit, but it was his victory at the German Grand Prix at the Nürburgring on August 4 that became legendary. In that race, Fangio beat Ferrari drivers Peter Collins and Mike Hawthorn in an exciting duel. With these victories, the Argentinian achieved his fifth and final World Drivers' Champion title, an unprecedented milestone that cemented his place among the greatest of all time.

In 1958, Fangio won his last race, the Gran Premio Ciudad de Buenos Aires, on February 3 in his homeland, before retiring from Formula 1 on July 6 at the Reims circuit, the place where he had debuted ten years earlier. It was an emotional moment that had come full circle for the Argentine pilot. Earlier that year, Fangio was kidnapped in Cuba by the group "26 de Julio," which prevented him from racing in the Cuban Grand Prix. This traumatic experience not only marked the end of his racing career but also highlighted the dangers and challenges he faced off the track.

The years after his retirement were full of tributes and recognition from the world of cinema, art, and motorsports. Although retired from racing, Fangio remained an iconic figure—a living legend. However, his health began to deteriorate slowly. In 1971, he suffered a heart attack that kept him hospitalized for weeks. The following year, he suffered a personal loss with the death of his father, Don Loreto, who had been his hero and mentor.

In 1982, at the age of 71, Fangio underwent heart surgery that left him in a delicate condition, but this did not prevent him from continuing to travel the world to attend the Grands Prix and accompany the new drivers in the arena. In 1992, at the age of 81, he underwent surgery to remove a benign tumor, which affected the functioning of his kidneys. Despite these challenges, Fangio continued to display his unbreakable spirit, even meeting Ayrton Senna in Buenos Aires during an event sponsored by the Brazilian driver, where both expressed mutual admiration and respect (Museo Juan Manuel Fangio, n.d.).

By 1995, Fangio's health continued to deteriorate. He was always accompanied by his closest relatives, such as his niece Ruth Fangio, his nephew Roland Verdier, and his wife Dolly. In his final days, he was briefly hospitalized under the watchful eye of Mercedes-Benz Argentina's highest officials. On June 24, he shared his last gathering with his family and friends to celebrate his birthday. Less than a month later, on July 15, the flu that turned into pneumonia forced him to be admitted to an emergency clinic due to respiratory problems.

Juan Manuel Fangio died on Monday, July 17 at 4:10 in the morning, surrounded by affection. His remains were guarded by an honor guard and veiled in the White Room of the Government House, the Argentine Automobile Club, and the next day in the Balcarce Museum. His funeral brought together thousands of people, a testament to the profound impact he had on the world of motorsports and on 20th-century Argentinian society, which adored him as a hero of the caliber of Diego Maradona. Finally, his remains were taken to the family pantheon in the cemetery of his hometown, along with his deceased parents and siblings, fulfilling his wish. This emotional moment occurred on July 18, with a heartbroken crowd paying tribute to a legend who had left an indelible mark on motorsports history (Motorsport, 1995).

The Resilient Champion

Juan Manuel Fangio's life was filled with moments that would have crushed a lesser spirit. But he was a man who understood that resilience wasn't just about enduring—it was about learning, evolving, and finding new paths when doors closed. His journey is full of stories that prove that even when the odds are stacked against you, there's always a way to push through.

I would now like to review the period of time that I consider key in his life: the early days. As we learned in his story, he didn't grow up with a silver spoon. In Balcarce, a small town surrounded by farmland, opportunities were as scarce as good roads. He had a knack for cars but driving them was a luxury reserved for the elite. Fangio had to make do with being a copilot and watching from the passenger seat as others took the wheel. It could have been discouraging, but instead, he took every moment as a lesson. When he wasn't helping with repairs, he observed how cars worked, paying attention to every detail.

He was patient while waiting for the chance to prove himself and knowing that even if the cars weren't his, the knowledge he gained was. It was the resilience to learn from whatever was available that would later define his success. Then there was the crash at Monza in 1952. Fangio had just won his first world championship and expectations were high. But as fate would have it, the accident left him with injuries that most thought would end his career. The European elite, already skeptical of a South American driver, saw it as the end of the road for him. But the boy from Balcarce didn't see it that way. He saw it as a call to prove himself once again.

When he returned to the track, he wasn't just racing against other drivers—he was racing against the doubts and assumptions that had followed him his entire career. It was his resilience that allowed him to turn a devastating setback into a comeback story for the ages.

The final turning point was Fangio's decision to retire. It takes a different kind of resilience to leave behind a life of success and triumph, to acknowledge that your journey has reached its end. Many struggle with the idea of retirement and feel lost and uncertain about what comes next, but Fangio showed that resilience also means knowing when to step away. He didn't cling to the past or try to reclaim his previous glory. Instead, he embraced the end of his racing career, allowing himself to explore new pursuits. Fangio's journey is a reminder that resilience is about adapting to the twists and turns of life. It's about finding strength in the face of adversity, learning from setbacks, and knowing when to move on. His story inspires us to face our challenges with courage and determination, proving that even when the road seems blocked, there's always a way through. As we reflect on his enduring legacy in Formula 1, we can see how his resilience continues to inspire future generations of drivers and serves as a beacon for anyone striving to achieve their own version of success.

Chapter 2:

Ayrton Senna—Determination

Determination is the tenacious drive to pursue goals despite obstacles, setbacks, and challenges. It is the fire within that keeps you moving forward when everything else urges you to give up. This virtue is what separates the mediocre from the great and the great from the legendary.

On the track, determination is what propels drivers to push their limits, keep striving for perfection, and never accept anything less than the best.

Ayrton Senna is the embodiment of this value.

Senna's approach to racing was characterized by his intense concentration and fierce competitiveness, which seemed to contrast with his humble and kind personality outside the car. From his early days in karting, he demonstrated an insatiable desire to win and a refusal to back down from any challenge. His determination was not just about winning races, but the relentless pursuit of excellence and a performance as fierce as elegant. Senna's drive to be the best propelled him to achieve extraordinary feats in Formula 1, earning him three World Championships and a legacy that continues to inspire drivers and fans alike. Through his story, we see how determination invariably leads to success. Understanding success as a set of factors that are not limited to the recognition of others, but to the internal certainty of having conquered and defeated oneself once again.

The Legend Emerges

The legend of Brazilian motorsports came into this world on March 21, 1960, in a regional hospital in tropical São Paulo (Traducciones, 2021). Son of Milton da Silva, an automotive businessman who owned land and factories, and Neide Joanna Senna da Silva, who came from a family of Italian descent. Ayrton had an older sister, Viviane, and a younger brother, Leonardo.

The house where he lived during his first four years was located less than 330 feet from the Campo de Marte, a place where the

Aeronautical Material Park and an airport operated. At the young age of 3, Senna showed motor difficulties and had trouble climbing stairs.

Milton saw inexhaustible energy in his son. Maybe that's why, when Senna was 4 years old, he built him a handmade kart, a machine made with a cane harvester engine that reached almost 40 mph. For a restless and curious child like Senna, it was more than a toy—it was the beginning of something extraordinary.

Senna was an athletic child, and in addition to karting, he was good at gymnastics and other sports. At age 7, he learned to drive a Jeep on his family's farm and shift gears without using the clutch. The family affectionately called him "Beco," and although his motor problems persisted, his driving skills were remarkable. Thus it was that young Ayrton soon demonstrated his skill behind the wheel. He began driving a professional kart, although without officially competing. It was at the age of 11, in the rain, when he made his first lap on a circuit, and his ability left everyone amazed. The following year, he took his kart apart to understand how it worked and how he could make it faster, demonstrating a natural inclination for mechanics and a determination to perfect his technique. This early curiosity and dedication indicated that Senna was not just a kid playing with a kart—he was cultivating the skills that would lead him to become one of the most iconic drivers in history.

Senna also showed his determination in academics. He attended Rio Branco School in the Higienópolis neighborhood of São Paulo and graduated in 1977, earning good grades in physics, mathematics, chemistry, and English. He then enrolled in a college specializing in business administration but dropped out after three months to concentrate on his racing career (Traducciones, 2021). Although he did well academically, his true interest was on the slopes.

When Ayrton was just 9 years old, his father bought him his first kart, previously owned by Emerson Fittipaldi. This kart, weighing under 110 pounds and equipped with hydraulic disc brakes, could reach speeds over 60 mph. Senna's debut race took place in a parking lot at Campinas, where he competed against many older drivers between 18 and 20. The starting positions were determined by drawing lots, and Senna pulled the number one, earning his first pole position. His smaller size and lighter weight gave him an early advantage, allowing him to lead the pack. However, after 15 laps, he was overtaken, and with just 3 laps left, an unfortunate incident occurred. He was in third place when another driver made contact with his rear wheel, causing him to flip over. It was his first karting race and he couldn't finish.

By July 1, 1973, 13-year-old Senna was ready for his first official race at the Winter Tournament at Interlagos, driving kart number 42 (Senna, 2023). He won both of his races convincingly, signaling the start of a remarkable career. A week earlier, his father had hired Lucio Pascoal Gascon, a Spanish military mechanic nicknamed "Tchê," to be Senna's personal kart mechanic. Tchê had previously worked with Fittipaldi and José Carlos Pace, and his partnership with Senna continued throughout the entirety of Senna's karting career, even accompanying him to Formula Ford in England.

In that race, despite being the youngest driver on the grid, he showed exceptional confidence and control. During the race, Senna led most of the time, challenging much older and more experienced drivers. This first triumph was just the beginning of a career marked by success and determination.

The young Senna had to wait until the following year, 1974, to win his first major championship, the Paulista Championship in the junior category (Senna, 2023). That year, he competed with number 42 and showed that he had the talent to go far.

A year later, Senna became the Paulista champion in the 100 cm³ category and was the Brazilian runner-up, in addition to obtaining an outstanding second place in the Itacolomy Tournament in the junior category. In 1976, Ayrton repeated as the Paulista champion, keeping the number 42. He also achieved third place in the Brazilian championship, won the Three Hours of Karting, and was the Paulista runner-up in the 100 cm³ category.

However, what really set Senna apart was his willingness to work hard and continually improve. After losing a race due to rain, he spent several days practicing in those conditions until he perfected his technique. This level of commitment and determination was not common in drivers his age and reflected his desire to reach the top.

Thus, the first years of his career as a driver were marked by triumphs and conquests. With his motor skills already well cultivated, the young Brazilian dreamed big and wanted to become a Formula 1 driver.

Senna's karting career was impressive. In 1977, he won the South American Karting Championship, and between 1978 and 1982, he participated in the World Karting Championship, finishing as runner-up on two occasions. During this time, he had as a teammate Terry Fullerton, a driver that Senna greatly respected because of his ability and because, in karting, there was not the politics or money that he saw in the largest competitions. For him, those years were key to developing his skills and his ability to drive in adverse conditions.

Senna's determination led him to make bold decisions. At 18, he left Brazil to move to Europe and compete in the World Karting Championship. It was a risky leap, but young Ayrton knew that to be the best, he had to face the best. In 1978, he joined the Italian DAP team, competing in the world karting championship and finishing as runner-up in 1979 and 1980.

Throughout these years, Senna perfected his ability to drive in the rain, a quality that would identify him throughout his entire career and showed impressive consistency.

In 1981, Senna began competing in the British Formula Ford 1600, where he won the championship in his first year. Although this category was not as well known as Formula 1, it was a crucial step in his career, allowing him to demonstrate his talent and attract the attention of sponsors and Formula 1 teams. During this time, Senna had to deal with financial challenges and pressure to join the family business. But his determination to continue racing led him to return to England to take part in Formula Ford 2000, where he also won the British and European championships in 1982.

After his successes in Formula Ford, Senna moved to British Formula 3 in 1983, competing with the West Surrey Racing team. It was here that Senna cemented his reputation as an exceptional driver. He dominated the first half of the championship but faced a close battle with Martin Brundle, who was also destined to make it to Formula 1. Senna won the championship in the final round, securing his place among Europe's best young drivers.

These achievements in Formula Ford and Formula 3 earned him the opportunity to test Formula 1 cars for teams such as Williams, McLaren, Brabham, and Toleman. Although he could not find a place in the bigger teams, Senna debuted in Formula 1 in 1984 with the modest Toleman team, where his talent and determination became clear to everyone. His entry into Formula 1 marked the beginning of a career that would lead him to become a legend, but his history in karting and the minor categories showed that success is always built on the basis of determination and passion for motorsports.

In Search of Glory

After winning five British championships in just three years, Ayrton abandoned a future in his father's business and left behind a young marriage to pursue success in Formula 1.

In 1983, his debut in Formula 1 was with the Toleman team, where he became Johnny Cecotto's teammate. The legend's World Championship debut took place at the 1984 Brazilian Grand Prix, held on his home soil. In his first race, he qualified 16th out of 26 but failed to finish the race (Donaldson, 2019). However, in the next race, the South African Grand Prix at Kyalami, Senna showed his potential by earning his first points in Formula 1 by finishing in 6th position. Senna repeated this result at the Belgian Grand Prix, demonstrating his ability to quickly adapt to the new level of competition.

The young promise's true revelation of the season came at the Monaco Grand Prix. In this race, he started from the 13th position on the grid and, in extremely wet conditions, showed an extraordinary ability to push through the field, passing car after car on the tight Monaco circuit.

By then, Senna was already known for his fierce ambition and desire to win at any cost. It was this attitude that led him to challenge the limits and himself and often earned him criticism from his rivals and observers. Realizing that Toleman's resources were limited for his ambition, Senna bought out his contract, and in 1985, he moved to Lotus, where in three seasons, he achieved 16 pole positions and six victories. This period also saw the increasingly intense rivalry between Senna and Prost, two of the best drivers of the time.

The Lotus proved to be a fast car throughout the season, but its reliability left much to be desired. Over the next seven races, Senna failed to score points, largely due to mechanical problems. Despite these ups and downs, Senna had gained popularity in the Lotus team, but his teammate, Angelis, was unhappy with what he perceived as favoritism toward Senna, and eventually left the team at the end of the season.

In 1986, Senna was leading the championship, but the car's poor reliability soon began to affect his results. Although he finished on the podium seven times after Portugal and won another race in Detroit, he was not enough to compete for the world title.

It was 1988, and the Brazilian was hungry for more glory. He joined the McLaren team, signing a three-year contract and teaming up with two-time world champion Alain Prost. This union marked the beginning of one of the most famous rivalries in the history of Formula 1.

Nineteen eighty-eight was a tense year between Senna and Prost. Their rivalry intensified, with battles on the court and psychological games off it. On September 25, at the Portuguese Grand Prix, the first major incident between the two drivers occurred. At Estoril, Senna had a slight advantage in the overall championship standings, but the rivalry reached a new level when Senna, after being overtaken by Prost, performed an extremely dangerous maneuver near the wall on the finish straight. The action surprised Prost, who managed to win the race but was shocked by Senna's aggressiveness. This incident left a mark on the relationship between both drivers, as Prost began to see Senna as a reckless competitor.

Prost expressed concern about Senna's conduct on the track. "Senna has a little problem. He thinks he can't kill himself because he believes in God in all those things, and that's very dangerous," Prost commented (Dagless, 2023).

Despite these tensions, the rivalry did not prevent McLaren from achieving success. That year, Senna and Prost competed fiercely for the title, with Senna eventually winning the championship after an impressive victory at the Japanese Grand Prix. Senna shared his feelings after his first world title (Dagless, 2023):

> I managed to remove the thorn that was stuck in me, get rid of that emptiness, the desire for victory. Now I want to improve as a person. I am only 28 years old and my whole life ahead of me.

The year 1989 was the turning point in the relationship between Senna and Prost. At the San Marino Grand Prix, the tension boiled over. They had agreed that whoever reached the first corner first would retain the position, but after a red flag following an accident by Gerhard Berger, Prost overtook Senna at the restart of the race. Senna counterattacked and regained the position, which angered Prost. Jo Ramírez, McLaren team manager at the time, recalled that Prost refused to get on the podium and left the circuit. "I tried to convince him to stay because they were going to fine him. He told me that he preferred the fine because if he stayed so angry he was going to say something he was going to regret," Ramírez said (Martin, 2023). Reconciliation came at the end of the 1993 season when Prost won his fourth world championship and Senna invited him to the podium, symbolizing the closing of an era of intense rivalry.

Ayrton Senna is remembered for his ferocity on the track and his glory. It was to be expected that the Brazilian would make rivals with such a peculiar personality. So it was that toward the end of the race he met his last worthy opponent, the German Michael Schumacher. As Alain Prost and Nigel Mansell were leaving Formula 1, the German rookie emerged as the driver capable of challenging the Brazilian, leading fans to expect great duels in the years to come. Their rivalry was short but intense, leaving a deep impression in the history of Formula 1.

Senna was already a benchmark in Formula 1, with more than 35 victories, when Schumacher began to make his appearance on the scene. During the 1992 season, Schumacher began to show his competitiveness, challenging Senna on several occasions. In one race, Schumacher complained about Senna's tactics, as Senna was struggling to maintain his track position. Senna became enraged by the rookie's criticism and had a heated verbal confrontation with Schumacher (Watson, 2021).

At the 1992 French Grand Prix, Schumacher had an accident with Senna, which caused even more tension between the drivers. Schumacher admitted that the accident was his fault, but also commented that Senna came into the corner at high speed, leaving him little room to maneuver.

The last season in which Senna and Schumacher competed was in 1994, with Senna in Williams and Schumacher in Benetton. Although Williams' performance was superior, the car had stability problems, and Schumacher was a tenacious competitor. In the fateful Imola race, Senna was leading when he suffered an accident that ended his life.

Years later, when Schumacher became one of the most successful drivers in the history of Formula 1, he always recognized Senna's greatness and the deep sadness he felt for his tragic death. "Senna is the greatest," Schumacher said. "He cannot be compared to pilots of different eras, but he was unique" (Autosport, 2000).

Beyond Racing

The 1994 San Marino Grand Prix became a tragic weekend for Formula 1. During the first day of qualifying on Friday, Senna demonstrated his speed, but a serious accident involving young

Brazilian driver Rubens Barrichello shook the paddock. Senna's compatriot only suffered a broken nose and bruised ribs, but he was unable to continue the rest of the weekend. As Barrichello himself recalled, "The first face I saw was Ayrton's. He had tears in his eyes. I had never seen that in Ayrton before. I got the impression that he felt my accident as if it were his own" (A Tribute to Life Network, 2011).

The following day, Saturday, Roland Ratzenberger's tragic accident occurred during the qualifying session. Ratzenberger, in his third race, went off the track at 195 mph after his front wing failed, hitting the wall at the Villeneuve corner and returning to the track lifeless. Senna arrived at the scene of the accident but was stopped by the FIA's medical director, Professor Sid Watkins, who informed him that Ratzenberger was clinically dead. Senna began to cry. Watkins tried to console him by telling him to back off and "go fishing," but Senna refused (Haldenby, 2016).

Ratzenberger's accident was the first death in a Formula 1 event since the death of Elio de Angelis in 1986, and the first in a race since Riccardo Paletti in 1982. This event shook the entire Formula 1 community and deeply affected Senna. Although he initially decided not to participate in the race, he later changed his mind, intending to pay tribute to Ratzenberger by waving an Austrian flag if he won. On Sunday, before the race, Senna spoke to his fellow drivers, suggesting the formation of the Grand Prix Drivers' Association to address safety issues.

In the race, Senna took the lead from the beginning, but on the seventh lap, the fatal accident occurred at the Tamburello curve. The car went off the track at 190 mph and hit the wall, causing catastrophic damage to the vehicle and Senna himself. The right front wheel came off and hit Senna's helmet, causing fatal skull fractures. Another component of the car penetrated the helmet, causing a wound to the forehead and damaging the brain. Although he received immediate medical attention and was taken by helicopter to the Maggiore Hospital in Bologna, his injuries were too serious and he died that same day.

The news of Senna's death shocked the world of motorsport and beyond. Senna's funeral was held in São Paulo, attracting millions of people and important motorsport figures such as Alain Prost, Gerhard Berger, and many other drivers. It was a massive farewell for one of the most beloved and talented drivers in Formula 1's history.

The inscription on his tombstone reads, *"Nada pode me separar do amor de Deus,"* meaning "Nothing can separate me from the love of God," a reminder of Ayrton Senna's spiritual and human legacy.

Beyond his skill as a driver, Senna was known for his captivating personality. Despite his thin appearance, he had a powerful physical presence, and when he spoke, his words resonated with intensity. With his warm eyes and passionate voice, Senna could captivate an audience, and his magnetism transcended the track. Even at press conferences, the other pilots and journalists listened to him attentively because his words were full of irresistible energy.

Senna lived every moment with unwavering passion, not only on the track but also in his daily life. His teammates and rivals acknowledged his dedication but some also questioned his methods, suggesting that his unbridled ambition sometimes brought him to the brink of danger. Martin Brundle, a driver and commentator, said of Senna: "I define a genius as someone who is just on the edge of sanity. Senna was like that, on the edge of madness, but right on the edge" (A Tribute to Life Network, 2018).

Even Senna acknowledged that he sometimes went too far. In qualifying for the 1988 Monaco Grand Prix, Senna, already on pole, continued to push until he was more than two seconds faster than Prost. "Suddenly, I was scared," Senna confessed, "because I realized it was so far beyond my conscious understanding" (de Menezes, 2014).

Senna was also aware of his mortality and used fear to keep his limits in check. His vision of motorsport was more than a competition. For him, racing was a metaphor for life and a means to discover himself. Despite this intense self-exploration, Senna had a deep sense of humanity and cared for those less fortunate. He donated millions of his personal fortune to help needy children in Brazil, proving that his commitment to motorsports was not his only passion.

Ayrton Senna's life and career were a constant search for glory, with moments of triumph and tragedy that left a deep impression on the history of Formula 1 and on all those who were lucky enough to know him.

Chapter 3:

Bruce McLaren—Vision

Vision is the unique capacity to see beyond the immediate and imagine a reality that does not yet exist. It's the force that drives us to reach for something greater than ourselves. It's the trait that allows individuals to turn dreams into concrete actions, to create and innovate in ways that can transform industries and leave lasting legacies. This power to envision is the cornerstone of success for many leaders, and few have embodied this virtue as profoundly as Bruce McLaren.

He had a unique vision for what a racing team could become. In a sport where the margins between success and failure are razor-thin, his ability to see beyond the present and craft a strategy that pushed the boundaries of technology and teamwork made him a pioneer. McLaren's vision led to the creation of a racing team that would go on to achieve incredible success, laying the groundwork for a legacy that endures to this day.

McLaren's vision was about promoting a spirit of creation and collaboration that transcended the racetrack. This ethos has continued to inspire generations of engineers, drivers, and racing enthusiasts. His story teaches us that vision is not limited to a particular field or industry. It is a universal principle that can guide anyone toward greatness.

We will see how with determination, creativity, and resilience, we can turn our dreams into reality. His legacy encourages us to pursue our passions with unwavering focus and to never lose sight of the bigger picture. In this chapter, we explore how McLaren's vision shaped the world of motorsport and how it can inspire us all to envision a future filled with endless possibilities.

A Racing Prodigy

On August 30, 1937, Bruce McLaren was born in Auckland, New Zealand, who would become a motorsports legend and whose name would resonate, to this day, with great weight and honor (McLaren Racing, n.d.). Bruce McLaren grew up in a family whose passion for automobiles was palpable. His father, Les McLaren, ran a mechanic's workshop and service station on Remuera Road, a place that would soon become Bruce's learning ground. Since he was a child, Bruce showed a notable interest in everything related to cars. He was often seen in his father's shop, watching the mechanics at work and making friends with customers who passed by. This allowed him to develop an intuition for how cars work and develop his love for motorsports.

Bruce proved to be an active and energetic child, participating in various sports, such as rugby, where he became captain of his team. However, at the age of 9, his life took an unexpected turn when he was diagnosed with Perthes disease, a hip disorder that caused him great pain and forced him to remain immobile (McLaren Racing, n.d.). Thus, he spent several months in bed, unable to lead a life consistent with a child his age. This diagnosis was a great challenge for Bruce, who had to spend two years at the Wilson Home for children with physical disabilities in Takapuna, far from his hometown. During that time, he was in a wheelchair and later on crutches, which prevented him from playing rugby and limited his physical activities.

Despite the difficulty of his situation, Bruce did not let his disability define him. At the Wilson Home, he developed skills in other sports, such as rowing, and found ways to stay busy and positive despite physical restrictions. When he was finally able to walk again, albeit with a slight limp, his enthusiasm for motorsports intensified. He returned to spending time in his father's shop, where he learned about mechanics, engine building, and automobile repair. This hands-on environment and his father's encouragement fostered his growing interest in racing.

Bruce received his first driving experience at age 14 when his father restored an Austin 7 Ulster for him (Lyons, n.d.). With this car, he participated in his first hillclimb race, where he began to demonstrate his driving skills and his determination to compete. His family, especially his father, encouraged him to follow his passion, and together they worked on his physical recovery, technical skills, and driving.

Over time, Bruce began competing in local club events, and his talent for motorsports became evident. During his high school years, he studied at Seddon Memorial Technical College, where he excelled in engineering, which complemented his practical shop experience. This combination of formal education and practical training allowed Bruce to develop a deeper understanding of cars and racing.

The real opportunity for Bruce would come in 1957 when he participated in the New Zealand Grand Prix, a renowned race on the local circuit. Although he did not win, his performance caught the attention of Jack Brabham, an Australian driver with a solid reputation in the racing world. This meeting with Brabham would be decisive for Bruce, as it opened the door to new opportunities in elite motorsport. Bruce's outstanding performance also impressed the New Zealand International Grand Prix Association, which selected him for the "Driver to Europe" program. This program offered scholarships to New Zealand drivers to compete in Europe, where they could take on the best drivers in the world. Bruce McLaren was the first recipient of this scholarship, marking the beginning of his international career (Lyons, n.d.).

It was the following year, 1958, that Bruce traveled to the old continent to join the Cooper team and begin competing in Formula 2. During his first season, he competed in the German Grand Prix at the Nürburgring, where he finished fifth overall and first in the Formula 2 category. This impressive result led him to join Cooper's Formula 1 team, working alongside Brabham, who had by then become his mentor. It was the beginning of a new stage in Bruce's career, where he would demonstrate his talent and abilities in a more competitive arena.

In 1959, Bruce McLaren won his first Formula 1 race at the United States Grand Prix in Sebring, Florida, becoming the youngest driver to win a Formula 1 race at that time. This achievement not only cemented his position in the racing world but also allowed him to gain confidence for the next challenges. Bruce's success continued throughout the 1959 season, with several podiums and a third-place finish at the British Grand Prix, allowing him to finish sixth in the World Drivers' Championship.

During this time, Bruce also experienced major changes in his personal life. He married Patricia Yvonne Broad, a beauty specialist from Christchurch, and together they had a daughter, Amanda. The family settled in Walton-on-Thames, in Surrey, where Bruce built their home and continued to develop his career.

In 1960, Bruce McLaren continued to demonstrate his skill and talent in Formula 1, winning the Argentine Grand Prix at the start of the season. His outstanding performance allowed him to take the title of runner-up in the World Drivers' Championship, only behind his teammate Jack Brabham. However, the following seasons were not as fruitful in terms of success in Formula 1. Despite this, Bruce continued to compete in various categories and cemented his reputation as a versatile and talented driver.

In 1962, Bruce achieved one of his most memorable victories by winning the Monaco Grand Prix, a race known for its complexity and prestige. This victory was an important milestone in his career and established him as one of the best drivers of his time. During this time, Bruce also worked closely with the engineers and mechanics of the Cooper team. He was aware of the mechanical weaknesses of his car and wanted to use his knowledge and unstoppable curiosity to contribute to the evolution of the team that had seen him born in the world of motorsports.

Unfortunately, many of the political decisions made at the team's round table responded more to economic purposes than to the mechanical evolution of their cars. Against this backdrop, Bruce McLaren began to take significant steps toward his vision of building his own racing team in 1963. Although he was still racing for the Cooper team, he was also working on his own projects and designing sports cars. It was in that same year that he founded Bruce McLaren Motor Racing Ltd., a company dedicated to building and developing racing cars. Although this was the beginning of a new chapter for Bruce, he still had a long way to go to turn his vision into reality.

Throughout that year, and in parallel with his driving duties, Bruce dedicated himself to laying the foundations for his own racing team, while continuing to compete and obtain solid results for Cooper in Formula 1 and other categories. This entrepreneurial spirit and his commitment to excellence in motorsports would define the legacy of Bruce McLaren, who, with determination and creativity, would leave an indelible mark on the world of racing.

Founding McLaren Racing

McLaren Cars would change the face of motorsport forever. As a talented and visionary driver, McLaren wanted to create a racing team that could compete at the highest level while developing innovative and revolutionary cars. Bruce had already demonstrated his talent as a driver and builder, but now he embarked on an adventure that would require not only his skill behind the wheel but also his technical acumen and his vision for the future.

McLaren Cars' first creation was the McLaren M1A, a sports car designed to compete in the Can-Am championship (Philadelphia, n.d.). The M1A was an immediate success, demonstrating Bruce's ability to design and build competitive cars. With only 24 models manufactured, the M1A marked the beginning of a series of innovations that would define McLaren for years to come.

The next step for McLaren was the construction of the M1B, which brought the team into Can-Am and proved to be a formidable contender. McLaren, as a driver and constructor, showed his dedication to excellence and his willingness to face challenges. In 1966, the M1B allowed McLaren to win 43 races in the Can-Am season, surpassing rivals such as Porsche. This success cemented McLaren's reputation as an innovative and winning team.

In parallel to his success in Can-Am, Bruce McLaren was also working on building Formula 1 cars. In 1965, McLaren's first Formula 1 car, the M2B, debuted at the Monaco Grand Prix. Although the car did not have a great immediate impact, it laid the foundation for McLaren's entry into Formula 1, where Bruce had high hopes of success.

The year 1966 was crucial for McLaren, as it was then that Bruce and Chris Amon won the 24 Hours of Le Mans with a Ford GT40, in a thrilling finale that saw a triple victory for Ford (McLaren Cars, n.d.). This achievement confirmed Bruce McLaren as a talented driver and skilled builder, capable of success in one of the most prestigious races in the world.

However, it was in the Can-Am championship that McLaren showed his true dominance. In 1967, the team won five of six races, and in 1968, they won four of six. The peak came in 1969, when McLaren won every race of the season, establishing absolute dominance. The combination of Bruce's talents as a driver, designer, and engineer, along with teamwork and technical innovation, took McLaren to the top of Can-Am.

The year 1968 was also significant for McLaren, as Bruce won the Spa Grand Prix, his first victory in Formula 1 with a car of his own brand. This achievement was a milestone for the team and showed that the new team could compete at the highest level in Formula 1. From there, McLaren began to win more races, with Denny Hulme joining the team and achieving two additional victories in the season of 1968.

However, the road to success was not without difficulties. Bruce McLaren always faced technical and financial challenges as he developed his cars and maintained the team. As a leader, he had to balance his roles as driver, designer, and team manager, and his dedication to motorsport was unquestionable.

Tragically, Bruce McLaren's life was cut short prematurely on June 2, 1970, when he died in an accident while testing the new McLaren M8D at Goodwood Circuit in England (Hindle, 2024). During the test, the car's body came loose at high speed, causing the vehicle to lose stability and leave the track. The car crashed into a bunker being used as a signaling post, and Bruce died instantly from the impact. He was only 32 years old.

News of his death resonated throughout the motorsport world, with many left devastated by the loss of a man who was so much more than a talented driver. Bruce McLaren was a brilliant engineer, an innovative designer, and an inspiring leader. The tragedy left his team, McLaren Racing, in a state of shock. They had lost not only their founder and boss but also a friend and mentor.

However, Bruce McLaren's legacy and his vision for motorsport lived on. The McLaren team, although hit by tragedy, showed remarkable resilience and determination to continue the work Bruce had begun. Just twelve days after the fatal accident, two McLaren M8D cars were featured in the first Can-Am series race of that season in Canada. Denny Hulme, who had been a teammate and close friend of Bruce, participated in that race with his hands bandaged from burns suffered at the Indianapolis Grand Prix. In a touching tribute to Bruce McLaren, the team won that race, with Hulme finishing in first place.

The victory in Canada was more than a sporting triumph. It was a testament to the spirit and determination of Bruce McLaren, and the team's commitment to his legacy. This success inspired the team to continue and work hard to keep Bruce McLaren's vision alive.

Bruce McLaren's legacy lies not only in the continued success of the McLaren team in Formula 1 and other motorsport championships but also in his lasting influence on motorsport culture. Bruce was known for his work ethic, his dedication to technical improvement, and his philosophy that life should be measured by achievements and not just years lived. This attitude inspired many other drivers and teams to strive for excellence and not give up on challenges.

His imprint and heritage are also evident in the tradition of technical innovation that continues to characterize McLaren. The brand has remained at the forefront of automotive design and engineering, creating high-performance cars and always exploring new technological frontiers.

Legacy of Excellence

The early years of the McLaren Racing team were full of challenges and obstacles that tested the determination and vision of its founder and collaborators. From financial difficulties to technical problems and failures on the track, the road to success was not easy. By founding Bruce McLaren Motor Racing in 1963, McLaren began the transition from driver to constructor. It was not a trivial change since he had to design, build, and test his cars. This process involved enormous technical challenges, as it required not only knowledge and experience in automotive engineering but also the ability to manage a team and coordinate multiple tasks at the same time.

One of the first challenges McLaren faced was financing. Founding a racing team in the 1960s that met the expectations of the International Automobile Federation and the standards of the World Tour required a considerable investment, and Bruce McLaren did not have that financial backing. For nearly two decades, he had to rely on limited resources and struggled to find sponsors who shared his vision. Despite these limitations, McLaren managed to build his first cars and compete in some of the most prestigious races in the world.

As for the technical challenges, there were many obstacles to overcome to design and build competitive cars.

One of the first challenges was the chassis design. McLaren and his team had to create structures that were light but strong, capable of withstanding the intense forces generated by high-performance engines. This required high-quality materials and a detailed understanding of aerodynamics. For his car's debut in the Formula 1 championship, McLaren chose the M2B, which featured an innovative chassis made of lightweight materials but faced reliability and performance issues. The prototype debuted at the 1966 Monaco Grand Prix (Hindle, 2024).

The choice of engine was also a crucial technical challenge. McLaren had to find engines that were powerful and reliable, and that could be integrated into their chassis efficiently. McLaren's first engines came from Serenissima, an Italian company, but they proved to be less powerful than necessary to compete in the demanding environment of Formula 1. This limited the car's performance and affected the team's success in its early years.

Furthermore, consolidating a new team in a context as competitive as Formula 1 posed logistical challenges. McLaren had to hire engineers, mechanics, and other specialists to build and maintain his cars. He also needed infrastructure for development and testing, as well as sponsors and financing to sustain the team over the long term.

The competitive environment of Formula 1 meant that McLaren was not only competing against other established teams but also had to continually innovate to stay ahead. The pressure to produce immediate results was intense, and McLaren had to prove that his team was capable of competing with the best in the world.

Amid these difficulties, the McLaren Racing team also faced challenges on the track. In its early years, the team suffered numerous racing failures and retirements, which affected the team's morale and confidence. However, Bruce McLaren's legacy as a leader was crucial in keeping the team united and motivated. His charisma and ability to inspire others helped the team stay focused on their long-term goals, despite temporary setbacks.

Bruce McLaren's legacy serves as a source of inspiration for those seeking to achieve their goals and dreams. His story demonstrates the importance of perseverance and dedication in achieving success. McLaren did not let financial difficulties, technical problems, or on-track defeats deter him from his vision. Instead, he used these challenges as opportunities to learn and improve.

The values that Bruce McLaren embodied are still relevant today. His legacy highlights the importance of resilience and creativity in overcoming obstacles. His commitment to excellence and desire to innovate has influenced generations of drivers and teams in the world of motorsports. His example teaches us that the path to success may be difficult, but with determination and a clear vision, even the greatest challenges can be overcome.

His story is a testament to the human ability to overcome adversity and achieve great things. Bruce McLaren's legacy reminds us that true success comes from dedication and commitment to excellence.

Chapter 4:

Michael Schumacher—

Leadership

Schumacher's story is that of a young man who dreamed big. It was not simply talent that drove him, but a combination of determination, humility, and discipline that led him to be one of the greatest Formula 1 drivers of all time. But beyond the victories and championships, what stood out was his ability to guide others, inspire his team, and bring out the best in everyone around him.

This chapter explores the essence of that leadership and how Schumacher embodied it in every race, in every training session, and in every decision he made. We will look at how his unwavering focus and work ethic not only earned him a place in the Hall of Fame but also left an indelible mark on Formula 1. His story is a lesson in how a leader can create a culture of excellence and how that spirit can transcend beyond the tracks and resonate in the lives of all of us.

As we walk the path of his story, his triumphs, and his mistakes, we will see how he bravely faced challenges and how his ability to inspire and motivate his team was crucial to his success. We'll look back at the key moments that defined his career and legacy and discover what we can learn from his leadership style. In the end, Schumacher's legacy is not just about motorsport—it is about the impact a leader can have on the world and how we can apply those lessons to achieve our own goals. In this chapter, Schumacher becomes a symbol of the power of leadership and what it means to have a vision and carry it out with passion and dedication.

The Rise of a Champion

Michael Schumacher, one of the greatest Formula 1 drivers of all time, had a modest and unassuming beginning. He was born on January 3, 1969, in Hürth-Hermülheim, a suburb near Cologne, Germany (Hilton, 2007). His father, Rolf Schumacher, was a bricklayer and manager of the local kart circuit in Kerpen. Coincidentally, his mother, Elisabeth, worked in the circuit canteen. It was in that family environment where young Michael and Ralf, the youngest of the brothers, who would also later become a talented Formula 1 driver, developed their love for motorsports, although his first steps were rather small setbacks.

Like any child his age, Michael enjoyed playing with toys, but his father decided to give him a special gift: a pedal kart. It didn't take long until the humble device became the favorite object for the young Schumacher, who pedaled the kart at full speed, tracing rings on the grass in the backyard of his house. Rolf, seeing his son's passion for speed, decided to install a small motorcycle engine in the kart. This innocent gesture led to an unexpected accident, as Michael, inexperienced in controlling a motorized kart, crashed into a light pole. Fortunately, the accident was not serious, and young Michael did not seem alarmed when he discovered the danger associated with speed.

His passion was beginning to shine. He spent every free moment at his father's kart circuit, watching the more experienced drivers and practicing on his own kart. As he grew older, his skill and dexterity became evident to everyone around him. At the age of 6, he won his first kart championship, a remarkable achievement for someone so young. His parents, although they did not have many financial resources, were determined to support their son's emerging talent.

The Schumacher family was of modest means, but the karting community, which knew of Rolf and Elizabeth's efforts to nurture the little one's passion, was willing to help a young man with so much potential. Rolf and Elisabeth found local sponsors who believed in Michael's talent and were willing to fund his progression in motorsport. With this support, Michael was able to compete in larger karting tournaments, gaining experience and reputation as he progressed.

In 1987, when Michael was 18, he won both the German and European karting championships, cementing his place as one of the most promising young talents in European motorsport (Allen, 2000). Two years earlier he had managed to become runner-up in the world championship in the junior karting category. This success led him to make an important decision in his life: leave his studies to dedicate himself full-time to motorsports. Although he initially worked as an apprentice auto mechanic, his dedication and talent soon led to full-time employment as a racing driver.

As his career took off, Michael began to attract the attention of top racing teams. His aggressive but controlled driving style, combined with his dedication and work ethic, made him a leading figure in the world of karting. By then, he had not only learned to master the art of driving but also the importance of teamwork and mechanical preparation, skills that would later be crucial in his Formula 1 career.

It was in 1991 when the most anticipated moment for the German driver would arrive: his debut in Formula 1 (Collings, 2005). Eddie Jordan, the representative of the Jordan Grand Prix team, called him to replace Belgian driver Bertrand Gachot, who could not participate in the Grand Prix of Belgium due to legal problems. Despite being a rookie, Schumacher surprised everyone with his performance, qualifying in seventh place and showing a level of skill unusual for a driver outside of Formula 1. Although his run ended early due to mechanical problems, Schumacher had left a lasting impression, leading Benetton team boss Flavio Briatore to hire him for the rest of the season.

It was under this team that the young Schumacher began to cement his reputation as one of the most talented and promising drivers of his generation. In 1992, he took his first victory at the Belgian Grand Prix, plus eight additional podiums, leading him to finish third in that year's drivers' championship. Over the next few years, Schumacher demonstrated his ability to work with the team and achieve impressive results.

The following season was difficult for Benetton, which faced countless technical challenges. The title of Champion had to wait until the following year: 1994. That was a tragic year for Formula 1. During the San Marino Grand Prix, in Imola, the accident that caused the death of Ayrton Senna shocked the world of motorsports. Schumacher, who was competing in that race, witnessed the fateful accident in which his friend and hero lost his life. That season, Schumacher won his first Formula 1 World Drivers' Championship.

Although they were sworn rivals, Schumacher and Senna respected each other. The young German particularly admired the Brazilian. Despite his differences, Michael honored his teammate and worthy rival every time he had the opportunity.

In 1995, Schumacher defended his title successfully, winning nine races and earning 102 points, 33 more than his closest competitor, rival Damon Hill. It was the last year that Schumacher raced for Benetton before joining Ferrari in 1996 (Henry, 1998). This move marked the beginning of a new era for the Italian team, which had not won a world drivers' championship since 1979.

The first few years with Ferrari were challenging for Schumacher, as the team faced technical and performance problems. Despite this, Schumacher achieved some impressive victories and maintained his reputation as a talented and competitive driver. In 1997, his career had a controversial moment when he intentionally collided with Jacques Villeneuve in the European Grand Prix, leading to his disqualification and voiding of all his championship points.

In 1999, Schumacher suffered a serious accident at the British Grand Prix, breaking his leg and losing six races in the championship. Despite this, Ferrari won its first constructors' championship in 16 years. The year 2000 marked Schumacher's triumphant return, as he won his third drivers' championship after an intense duel with Mika Häkkinen and ushered in one of the most incredible eras of dominance in the sport's history.

From 2000 to 2004, Schumacher dominated Formula 1, winning five consecutive championships and setting records that remain unmatched. His mastery was so complete that many referred to this era as "the Schumacher era." His main rivals during this period were McLaren drivers Mika Häkkinen and David Coulthard, and Williams drivers Juan Pablo Montoya and Ralf Schumacher, his brother. During this stage of undeniable dominance, he received the mythical nickname "Kaiser," which means emperor in German, and by which the great champion is still referred to today.

In 2005 and 2006, Schumacher's lead began to fade as a new generation of drivers emerged, such as Fernando Alonso and Kimi Räikkönen. Schumacher battled performance and reliability issues in his car, but still demonstrated his skill and determination.

Finally, in 2006, after a successful and accomplished career, Schumacher announced his retirement from Formula 1. Throughout his career, he had achieved seven world championships, 91 victories, and numerous records that still stand today. Although his retirement marked the end of an era as an exceptional driver, Michael would not be away from the paddock for long.

The announcement of his return was received with great enthusiasm by motorsports fans, eager to see one of the most successful drivers in the history of Formula 1 return to action. His contract with Mercedes, initially for three years, had a significant impact on the world of Formula 1, revitalizing commercial and economic interest after the withdrawal of major manufacturers such as Honda, BMW, and Toyota in previous years.

However, Schumacher's return was not easy. Although at the 2010 Bahrain Grand Prix, he managed to qualify in seventh position and finished sixth, the start to the season was disappointing. In Melbourne, another seventh-place finish on the grid ended with Schumacher in tenth place after a collision with the then-dominant Fernando Alonso. The season continued to be difficult, with a retirement at Sepang due to mechanical problems and an incident at the Monaco Grand Prix, where Schumacher was penalized for overtaking Alonso with the safety car on track.

Throughout that season, Schumacher struggled to find his rhythm, with a final result of 72 points, compared to the 142 points of his teammate, Nico Rosberg. The following season did not show much improvement for Mercedes, although Schumacher achieved a stronger performance, approaching Rosberg's performance and earning a personal best fourth-place result (Donaldson, n.d.).

Schumacher's return to Mercedes in 2012 began with some difficulties, but throughout the year, his luck began to change. At the European Grand Prix, held in Valencia, he achieved his first podium since his return to Formula 1 in 2010, after six years without taking the podium. This achievement was an important milestone for Schumacher and an indication that he still had the potential to compete at the highest level.

However, the relationship between Schumacher and Mercedes was not easy. According to John Barnard, the team's engineer, the decline in Schumacher's performance after his first retirement was due, in part, to his driving style. Because of this, Mercedes AMG preferred Nico Rosberg, who, according to team officials, had a more understeering driving style, while Schumacher preferred cars with a greater tendency to oversteer. This lack of synchronization between the team and the driver affected Schumacher's performance on his return. In addition to the technical differences between the German and his team, Mercedes-Benz's announcement of the hiring of Lewis Hamilton for the 2013 season left Schumacher without a seat, and shortly after, he confirmed his definitive withdrawal from the competition. That season he would see it from afar. The "Kaiser" understood that his era had ended, and with the humility that characterized him, he was able to be happy to see the rookie Hamilton taking the first steps toward his era of dominance.

On December 29, 2013, an event occurred that would change the former pilot's life forever. Schumacher suffered a serious accident while skiing in the French Alps. The accident resulted in serious brain injuries and an induced coma that lasted several months. Fortunately, he managed to survive after being in intensive care for half a year. Schumacher has since been undergoing treatment and rehabilitation, but little is known about his current condition. His family has maintained strict control over his privacy in the last decade after the accident, revealing little information about his state of health, as they do not want the stimuli of public life to affect the "Kaiser's" recovery.

Some of those close to him have hinted that his health situation does not reveal considerable improvements and have even hinted that the most important motorsports legend of all time will no longer return to the public scene (Economic Times, 2024). Those of us who admire him for his masterful talent and eloquent personality will find no better way to honor him than by learning from his humility, commitment, and leadership. Thus, converting our own lives into a tribute to his greatness.

Legacy of Leadership

Michael Schumacher's legacy of leadership is something that resonates not only in the world of motorsport but also in the values of those who have been fortunate enough to work alongside him. The seven-time Formula 1 world champion was not only an exceptional driver but also a natural leader who understood the power of empathy, teamwork, and dedication to detail. These values, deeply rooted in Schumacher's work ethic, left an indelible mark on Ferrari and the entire sport.

One of the most notable characteristics of Schumacher's leadership was his ability to set a standard of excellence through his work ethic and positive attitude. Ross Brawn, who worked with Schumacher at Ferrari, recalled how the German driver was an example for the team, always willing to put in maximum effort. It was not unusual to see Schumacher working tirelessly, even in his spare time, to perfect his performance. This attitude carried over to the entire team, inspiring the engineers and mechanics to work with the same level of dedication and commitment (Woodhouse, 2022).

Schumacher also had a special gift for bringing people together and creating an atmosphere of camaraderie and respect. He never publicly criticized his team and always addressed any problems privately. This approach of not embarrassing anyone in public created an environment of trust and loyalty within the team. James Allison, who worked at Ferrari during Schumacher's time, described how this policy, also implemented by Jean Todt, allowed the team to focus on performance rather than internal politics (Woodhouse, 2022).

Additionally, Schumacher was known for his ability to connect with people on a personal level. He remembered birthdays, children's names, and other important details for his teammates. This type of attention to personal details demonstrated his genuine concern for the people with whom he worked. In his book *Survive. Drive. Win.* Nick Fry (2019) recounts how Schumacher was the first to text him when his son was sick, reminding him of the importance of family and offering his support. This empathy and consideration for others made people feel valued and motivated to do their best.

Schumacher's relationship with his teammates also reflected his ability to inspire and guide others. At Mercedes, where he returned to Formula 1 in 2010, Schumacher became a mentor to Nico Rosberg, his young teammate. Through advice and guidance, he helped Rosberg understand the importance of building strong relationships with engineers and adopting a more collaborative approach. This approach directly contributed to Rosberg's success in 2016, when he won the Formula 1 World Championship ahead of Lewis Hamilton.

Schumacher's leadership legacy extends beyond his time at Ferrari and Mercedes. Mattia Binotto, Ferrari's current team boss, credits Schumacher with teaching him what it means to be a leader (Woodhouse, 2022). From the start of his career in 1995, Binotto learned from Schumacher the importance of teamwork, patience, and perseverance. These lessons have been fundamental to the way Binotto runs Ferrari today.

Michael Schumacher's leadership was a product of his humility, respect for others, and unwavering work ethic. His ability to bring people together and motivate them to give their best was reflected in his success on the track and in the legacy he left at Ferrari and in Formula 1 in general. His example inspires us to pursue excellence by cultivating humility and self-questioning, and to seek collaboration and consensus with a clear objective.

His teaching is as great as his greatness. May this chapter and the work of this book serve as a tribute and gratitude to one of the leaders who have most inspired me.

Chapter 5:

Fernando Alonso—

Humbleness

Fernando Alonso is a name that evokes a sentiment of greatness in the world of Formula 1. Throughout his illustrious career, he has won two world championships and racked up numerous victories, but beyond his achievements on the track, it is his humility that sets Alonso apart from his contemporaries.

In a sport known for its strong egos and flamboyant personalities, Alonso's humility is a breath of fresh air, and his focused and respectful approach toward his teammates, rivals, and fans is an inspiring example.

The world of Formula 1 can be ruthless. Drivers compete at the limit and tensions are high. Their performance defines their value in the driver market and their exposure and behavior outside the paddock influence public opinion and, ultimately, their lives. In this sense, the ego emerges as a natural defense for those who must deal with the constant pressure and expectations of the entire community. But this defense can easily become a double-edged sword, and lead drivers to have arrogant and egotistical attitudes toward their teammates, followers, and, especially, rivals.

In an environment like this, Alonso shows that humility is not a sign of weakness, but of strength. His ability to keep a cool head and treat everyone with respect, from his teammates to his mechanics and rivals, has earned him the admiration of people inside and outside of the sport.

In this chapter, we will explore Alonso's life story, from his origins to his rise to the top of Formula 1 and come to understand how his experiences and values shaped his character. Through concrete examples, we will see how his humility allowed him to build strong relationships and earn the respect of his colleagues. We will also discuss how we can learn from Alonso and apply his lessons of humility in our own lives, remembering that true success is not measured only by trophies, but also by the positive impact we leave on others. We will discover how this value can be a source of strength and resilience, allowing us to achieve our dreams without losing sight of what really matters.

The Early Years

Fernando Alonso Díaz was born on July 29, 1981, in Oviedo, Asturias, into a family that valued humility and hard work. His father, José Luis Alonso, was a karting enthusiast and worked as an industrialist. He built the first kart for his son when Fernando was just 3 years old. Unlike his older sister, Lorena, who was not interested in karting, Fernando immediately felt attracted to the world of speed.

In an interview, Alonso recalled those early years and how his father transmitted his love for motorsports to him. "My father built a kart for my sister, but she didn't want anything to do with it. So I, when I was barely three years old, got into the kart and I loved it," Alonso said (Bautista, 2020). His father began taking him to a parking lot where he could practice, walking alongside him while Fernando drove.

Despite his young age, Fernando's talent soon became evident. At the age of 7, he had already won his first official karting race in the Asturias children's championship. It was an important moment for him and his family, and after that, Fernando and his father began to travel to competitions throughout Spain. José Luis acted as a mechanic and counselor, while Ana, Fernando's mother, worked to support the family.

Throughout those early years, Fernando Alonso stood out for his humility and calm approach. He was always a child who enjoyed school and spending time with his family. "I liked going to school and learning new things. I was always well prepared for exams," Alonso remembered in an interview (Bautista, 2020). But outside of school, his true passion was karting.

However, the road to success was not easy. The Alonso family did not have abundant resources and competing in the world of karting required significant investments. There were moments of doubt and financial challenges, but the unwavering support of his family kept Fernando's hope alive. In those early years, his father drove an old Peugeot while other competitors arrived in luxurious cars, but that did not stop Fernando from demonstrating his talent.

In those formative years, the young Fernando Alonso began to forge his humility and dedication. He won local championships in Asturias and Galicia, but always kept his feet on the ground. Although he sometimes competed against drivers who had more resources, he never let that get to him. "My father and I went to the races together, just the two of us. Other teams had trucks and entire teams, but we had a Peugeot and a kart," he recalled (Bautista, 2020).

One of the keys to Alonso's early success was his ability to establish meaningful relationships with key people in the karting world. One of those meetings was with Genís Marcó, a kart importer who was impressed by Fernando's skills. "My father and I were considering quitting karting because we couldn't afford to continue competing at that level. That's when Genís Marcó showed up and helped us," said the Spanish Champion (Marchi, 2023). With his support, the young Fernando had access to better karts and sponsors that allowed him to continue his career.

Success in karting led Fernando to compete in international championships, where he demonstrated his talent and his humility. At 14 years old, he was already the champion of Spain and Europe in the junior category, an achievement that allowed him to enter the International A category. In 1996, he was proclaimed junior world champion and began to attract the attention of other motorsports talents. In 1997, Adrián Campos, a former Formula 1 driver and manager, took an interest in him and became his mentor.

Over time, Alonso's humility became a fundamental part of his personality. Throughout his karting career, he never stopped being grateful to his family and those who supported him. He always remembered his roots and maintained a humble attitude, even when his career began to take off. As he said: "I will always be grateful to my family and everyone who helped me along my path. Without them, none of this would have been possible" (Bautista, 2020).

Reaching the Paddock

In 1999, the Formula 1 world began to take notice of the emerging talent of the young Asturian driver. Despite his youth, Alonso had already gained recognition in karting and junior categories, and he was ready to make the leap to Formula 1. His natural skill and dedicated approach to competition led to him being considered one of the brightest prospects in motorsport. That year, Alonso took a significant step by joining the Euro Open Movistar by Nissan team, managed by Adrián Campos, a former Formula 1 driver who became Alonso's mentor and manager. Campos played a crucial role in Fernando's career, helping him secure opportunities and guiding him through the complexities of professional motorsport. With Campos's guidance, Alonso competed in the Euro Open by Nissan, a European single-seater series that served as a launchpad for young talents toward higher categories (Formula 1, n.d.).

In this setting, Alonso quickly proved his worth by winning the first race of the season in Albacete. This was a crucial moment for the young driver, who was only 18 years old, and it was a clear sign that he was ready to compete at the highest level. Throughout the season, Alonso won eight of the fourteen races and was crowned champion, showcasing his talent and commitment to reaching the pinnacle of the sport. Even as his career took off rapidly, Alonso maintained his humility and dedication. He was known for his hard work, spending hours analyzing data and studying every detail of the car and the circuit. Unlike other drivers who preferred a more carefree attitude, Alonso was always focused on improving and learning. At that time, he lived in a modest accommodation in southern Spain, sharing space with other young drivers while concentrating on his training and development (Formula 1, n.d.).

In 2000, Fernando Alonso joined Formula 3000 International, a single-seater category considered the final step before Formula 1. He signed with the Astromega team and competed against other emerging talents, some of whom would also make it to Formula 1. Throughout that season, he demonstrated consistency and skill, achieving several podium finishes and ending the championship in fourth place, a remarkable position for a rookie. His talent did not go unnoticed by Formula 1 teams, who began to consider Alonso among their potential new drivers. Giancarlo Minardi, founder of the Minardi team, was on the lookout for young talent and saw Alonso's potential. At the end of 2000, Minardi offered Alonso a test with the team, giving the young driver his first experience in a Formula 1 car.

The test with Minardi was a pivotal moment for Alonso, as it opened the door for him to join the team as a regular driver for the 2001 Formula 1 season. Minardi was a small team with limited resources, but for Alonso, it was the perfect opportunity to prove his worth and determination. It was an opportunity he did not waste, and his performance that season caught the attention of larger, more established teams. In 2002, after his impressive debut with Minardi, Alonso was signed by Renault to serve as a test driver. Although this season did not offer many competitive opportunities, it served as a learning and adaptation year for Alonso, who made the most of every moment to hone his skills and familiarize himself with a high-level team environment.

Although Alonso regretted not being able to compete as a regular driver that year, he understood that it was part of the process and that it would prepare him for the 2003 season, where he would join the Renault team as an official driver, replacing Jenson Button. This transition marked the beginning of a period of growth and success for Alonso and the Renault team. That same season, Alonso made his debut with Renault at the Australian Grand Prix, where he achieved seventh place, earning his first Formula 1 points. It was just the beginning of a memorable season. At the Malaysian Grand Prix, Alonso became the youngest driver to achieve a pole position at just 21 years old, and he later took the podium, solidifying his position as an emerging star. Major figures in motorsport, like Schumacher, began to take notice when, still shy of media attention, the young Fernando Alonso walked through the paddock after putting on an unparalleled sports spectacle. That season also brought challenges for the young driver and his team, but these did not prevent him from achieving several more podiums, including a historic victory at the Hungarian Grand Prix, where he became the youngest driver to win a Grand Prix at the age of 22 years.

The following season was a period of consolidation for Alonso and Renault. Although he didn't win any races, he demonstrated consistency and skill by achieving several podium finishes and notable performances. Despite the ups and downs, Alonso maintained his focus and determination, even in challenging moments like the Monaco Grand Prix, where a collision with Ralf Schumacher prevented him from finishing the race while battling for the podium. The year 2005 was a turning point for Alonso. From the start of the season, he displayed impressive dominance, achieving several consecutive victories, including a memorable win at the Spanish Grand Prix, where he became the first Spanish driver to win his home

Grand Prix. This season also marked the beginning of the rivalry between Alonso and Michael Schumacher, who would be his main opponent for much of his career.

Alonso's consistency and ability to remain calm under pressure led him to win the 2005 Formula 1 World Championship, becoming the youngest driver to achieve this, at the age of 24 years. This victory was a significant milestone in Formula 1 history and a reflection of Alonso's exceptional talent. The year 2006 further solidified Alonso's position as one of the best drivers of his generation. Throughout the season, he faced challenges, including penalties and mechanical problems, but demonstrated his ability to overcome obstacles and stay calm in critical situations. But no adversity can stop a storm like Alonso, who capitalized on the challenges by turning them into his second Drivers' World Championship victory (Oporto, 2015).

A year later, with the conviction that new goals require sacrifices and changes, Alonso left Renault to join McLaren, a move that garnered much attention. However, his time at McLaren was tumultuous due to the rivalry with his teammate, rookie Lewis Hamilton. As the season progressed, the relationship between Alonso and McLaren became strained, with reports of internal discord and disputes over the treatment the drivers received. The conflict reached its peak during the Hungarian Grand Prix, where Alonso was penalized for blocking Hamilton during qualifying, affecting the team's dynamic. Additionally, 2007 was a year marked by the espionage scandal between McLaren and Ferrari. Although Alonso was indirectly involved in the controversy, he was not directly responsible for gathering information. At the end of the season, despite winning four races and finishing third in the drivers' championship, Alonso left McLaren due to internal tension and returned to Renault for 2008.

Alonso's return to Renault in 2008 was an attempt to regain the stability and success he had previously experienced with the French team. Although Renault was not at the competitive level of previous years, Alonso demonstrated his ability to get the most out of the car and achieve impressive results. In 2008, he won two Grands Prix, in Singapore and Japan, proving that he was still a world-class driver. However, the "Crashgate" scandal in Singapore, where it was revealed that his teammate, Nelson Piquet Jr., had intentionally crashed to benefit Alonso, tarnished part of his success (Coleman, 2023). Although Alonso was not involved in the conspiracy, the incident caused controversy and affected Renault's reputation.

In the following season, Renault's performance did not improve significantly, and Alonso, tired of the controversy and lack of transparency within the team and disagreeing with their strategic ethics, decided to seek new opportunities for 2010. It was then that he announced his move to Ferrari. Alonso's arrival at the Italian team was greeted with great enthusiasm, and expectations were high for the most coveted driver on the market. At Ferrari, Alonso found a team with the potential to compete for titles but also significant challenges. The 2010 season was one of the most exciting of the decade, with Alonso fighting for the championship until the final race in Abu Dhabi. Unfortunately, a strategic error in that race cost him the title, leaving him in second place behind Sebastian Vettel.

The following seasons, from 2011 to 2014, were a challenge for Alonso and Ferrari. Although he showed impressive consistency and achieved notable victories, Ferrari's car was not competitive enough to challenge Red Bull and their driver, Sebastian Vettel, who dominated those years. However, each race seemed to be taken as a personal challenge by the Asturian, who, against all odds, managed to get results far beyond expectations from the Italian team's car (Lifona, 2016). After leaving Ferrari in 2014, Alonso returned to McLaren, but the British team, which had partnered with Honda, suffered from numerous reliability and performance issues. Despite these difficulties, Alonso maintained a humble attitude and worked hard to get the best out of the car, demonstrating his determination and competitive spirit.

In 2015, McLaren-Honda struggled with technical issues and failed to be competitive. Throughout that season, Alonso demonstrated his professionalism and commitment to the team, despite constant mechanical failures and a lack of speed. During press conferences and interviews, Alonso maintained a respectful attitude and spoke about the importance of patience and teamwork to overcome difficulties. Even in the most frustrating situations, Alonso did not blame his teammates or show disdain; instead, he preferred to focus on building a better future for McLaren. At the end of the 2018 season, the double-world champion felt that a cycle had come to an end. It was time to give way to new talents showing conviction and determination. Once he officially retired, he dedicated himself to exploring other motorsport disciplines. During his retirement, Alonso maintained a humble attitude, thanking his fans for their constant support and emphasizing that his decision did not mean the end of his motorsport career, but the beginning of new adventures.

He competed and won in the 24 Hours of Daytona and the 24 Hours of Le Mans, besides competing in the World Endurance Championship with Toyota. He also participated in the Dakar Rally, demonstrating his versatility as a driver. He also participated in the Indy 500, an emblematic event in American motorsport, but failed to qualify for the race. His reaction to this setback was an example of his humility and sportsmanship. The Asturian was completely capable of acknowledging that he had failed and that he didn't feel prepared to run a race of this nature, as he had no experience in that part of motorsport. He smiled and thanked his team for their efforts, making it clear that failure is part of the learning process and does not determine one's value.

Eventually, Alonso's desire to compete in Formula 1 was rekindled, and in 2021, he announced his return to the category with Alpine, the successor team to Renault. His return was welcomed with enthusiasm, and Alonso expressed his gratitude for the opportunity to return to Formula 1 and work with a team that held a special place in his heart. During his time with Alpine, Alonso maintained his competitive spirit and demonstrated his ability to adapt to changes in the sport, which now included new faces and talents challenging his skills and career. In 2022, Alonso joined Aston Martin for the 2023 season and demonstrated that, despite his age and experience, he could still compete at the highest level. His humility continued to be a fundamental characteristic of his personality, and his focus on teamwork and respect for his teammates was evident. Even in press conferences and interviews, Alonso always spoke about the team's work and how everyone contributed to success, emphasizing the importance of humility and collective effort.

Off-Track Contributions

Off the track, Alonso has also been actively involved in charity events and activities, using his platform to contribute to charitable causes. To this day, he continues to demonstrate his commitment to social responsibility and his desire to make a difference in the community. This humility and willingness to help others reflect his character and personality, earning him the respect and admiration of fans and colleagues alike. In his personal life, Alonso has kept a low profile, focusing on his training and preparation for races. Despite his status as one of the most successful drivers in Formula 1 history, the Spaniard avoids ostentation and opts for a simple lifestyle centered on motorsport (The World Economic Forum, 2022). This humility and focus on hard work continue to be integral to his success, especially in his most recent stint with Aston Martin, where despite mechanical difficulties and the apparent fact that the English team struggles to compete with the dominant teams of the season, the double champion manages to keep showing us his skill, experience, and exceptional humanity.

Book Review Request

I'm so glad you're here, exploring the fascinating stories and personalities of Formula 1 with me. If you've found the insights and narratives in this book engaging, I'd love to hear your thoughts!

Leaving a review on Amazon will help others discover this unique perspective on the F1 paddock and encourage me to keep exploring and sharing these stories.

Whether it's a brief note about what resonated with you, a comment on your favorite chapter, or something else that stood out, I'd appreciate hearing from you. Sharing your thoughts doesn't have to be long or complicated—even a few words can make a big difference. Your review could be what inspires someone else to pick up this book and dive into the world of F1 strategy, passion, and competition.

If you've learned something new or enjoyed exploring these stories, would you consider leaving a review? I value your feedback, and I'm grateful for your support. Thank you for joining me on this journey, and I hope you continue to find inspiration and excitement as you turn the pages.

Chapter 6:

Lewis Hamilton—Perseverance

Perseverance is the ability to endure and also the willingness to learn, adapt, and grow from each challenge. It is the ability to transform setbacks into lessons, failures into opportunities, and moments of uncertainty into a reason to move forward with greater strength. Lewis Hamilton is a living example of how that radiance can illuminate the path to success and positive impact.

As one of the most successful drivers in the history of Formula 1, Hamilton has shown that success is not measured only in trophies and championships, but in the ability to overcome challenges and break barriers. This chapter explores how perseverance became the driving force of Hamilton's career, leading him to achieve astonishing achievements and leave a lasting mark on sport and society.

As we will see below, the history of the Englishman begins in a modest way.

As he advanced in his career, he faced discrimination and doubts about his ability in an environment that could be very hostile to anyone, especially a Black kid from the suburbs. But he never let those obstacles stop him. Every challenge he overcame, every prejudice he overcame, only strengthened his will. With each step forward, he overturned prejudices and changed perceptions, sowing a seed of diversity and respect that would pave the way for future pilots from lower social classes and belonging to marginalized social groups. His success on the track was not only measured in his great victories and impeccable titles but also in his courage to challenge the status quo and the inspiration he offered to other drivers from different backgrounds.

In this chapter, we will look at how Hamilton used his position to fight for diversity, inclusion, and social justice. His actions in and out of the car reflect a commitment to positive change, reminding us that each of us has the power to make a difference. As we explore Hamilton's life and career, we will learn how perseverance can be the key to transforming our own lives and leaving a mark on the world around us. Through his example, we will discover that the road to success can be steep and challenging, but with perseverance and determination, it is possible to achieve our goals and, at the same time, create a positive impact in our community.

Early Beginnings and Challenges

Lewis Hamilton was born on January 7, 1985, in Stevenage, Hertfordshire. His father, Anthony Hamilton, is from Grenada, while his mother, Carmen Larbalestier, is British, originally from Birmingham. This mix of backgrounds meant that Hamilton grew up in a family environment that celebrated diversity, but outside his home, he faced challenges and injustices related to his appearance from a young age. The resilience he developed during his childhood would be crucial for young Lewis in his sports career, where he took pride in being different in a sport where most faces didn't look like his (Hamilton, 2010).

Hamilton's parents separated when he was just two years old, and for most of his childhood, he lived with his mother and his two half-sisters, Samantha and Nicola. However, his life changed significantly at the age of 12 when he moved in with his father, his stepmother Linda, and his half-brother Nicolas, who would also pursue a career in professional racing. Raised as a Catholic, Hamilton led a relatively quiet life, but the challenges of family separation and a change of environment profoundly affected him.

Young Lewis found refuge from life's turmoil in sports. His father would later describe him as a restless and cheerful child (Eidell, 2024). At age 5, his father bought him a remote-controlled car, and the following year, he was already competing in the British Radio Car Association (BRCA) national championship, where he stood out by finishing in second place, competing against adults. This was an impressive achievement for someone so young, but his journey wouldn't be easy. As the only Black child competing in his club, Hamilton endured racist abuse, something he would have to learn to face with the help and support of his family.

At the age of 6, his father gave him a go-kart for Christmas and promised to support his career in motorsport as long as he worked hard in school. Anthony's commitment to his son's success was absolute; he left his job as an IT manager to work as a contractor and often juggled up to four jobs to finance his son's karting career. He sold double-glazed windows, washed dishes, and even put up signs for real estate agents, all while attending Lewis's races and providing the emotional support he needed.

Hamilton's education took place at the John Henry Newman School, a Catholic school in Stevenage. To protect himself from school bullying, he took karate classes starting at age 5. The young boy also faced difficult times at school, like when he was expelled due to a case of mistaken identity after a violent incident where it was thought he had attacked a classmate. The stigma was overwhelming, but young Hamilton found solace and happiness in sports. He played soccer for his school's team alongside future professionals like Ashley Young and was a devoted Arsenal fan.

Lewis Hamilton's motorsport career began in 1993 when he was only 8 years old (Benson, n.d.). It was then that he first got into a kart, and his natural talent became immediately evident. Soon, the promising young driver started winning races and championships in the cadet category, displaying a skill and focus that stood out among his competitors. Just two years later, at the age of 10, he became the youngest driver to win the British Cadet Karting Championship, an impressive achievement that put him on the radar of the motorsport community.

That same year, 1995, Hamilton had a key moment that would shape the course of his career. During the Autosport awards ceremony, he approached the head of the McLaren Formula 1 team, Ron Dennis, to ask for an autograph. It was then, with the confidence of a child who knows what he wants, that

Hamilton said, "Hi, I'm Lewis Hamilton. I won the British Championship, and someday I want to race with your cars." Dennis, impressed by the young driver's audacity, wrote in Hamilton's autograph book, "Call me in nine years; we'll work something out." Although it was only an informal promise, it was the beginning of a connection that would later prove crucial for Hamilton's career (Hamilton, 2010).

To young Lewis's joy, he had to wait much less. Three years after that encounter, in 1998, Ron Dennis fulfilled his promise and called Hamilton after the young driver won his second title in the Super One series and the British Championship. Dennis offered Hamilton a spot in McLaren's driver development program, with the option of a future position in Formula 1. This made Hamilton the youngest driver to secure a contract that would eventually lead him to Formula 1.

Hamilton continued to advance quickly in the Intercontinental A, Formula A, and later Formula Super A karting categories. In 2000, he became European champion with the highest points, solidifying his reputation as one of the most promising drivers of his generation. During this time, he shared a team with Nico Rosberg, who would later also reach Formula 1 with the Williams and Mercedes teams. The friendship and healthy rivalry between Hamilton and Rosberg grew. Neither of the two young drivers could have imagined the remarkable future that awaited them in the paddock and that they would experience it together.

Hamilton's karting career also led him to compete against some of motorsport's great names. In 2001, the great Michael Schumacher made an occasional return to kart racing, participating in an event where Hamilton and other future Formula 1 drivers like Vitantonio Liuzzi and Nico Rosberg also competed. At just 16 years old and with his racing career in its infancy, Hamilton finished seventh in the final, four places behind Schumacher. The seven-time world champion was so impressed by the young Briton's masterful skills that he publicly praised his race mentality and predicted a bright future for him (Formula 1, 2023; Christensen, 2022).

That same year, Lewis began studying at the Cambridge Arts and Sciences, a private secondary school in Cambridge, continuing his academic training while pursuing his passion for racing.

With his meteoric rise in karting, the British Racing Drivers' Club recognized Hamilton's potential and named him a "Rising Star," an honor reserved for young drivers with a brilliant time ahead (Christensen, 2022). Hamilton had demonstrated that he had the talent, courage, and perseverance to go far in motorsport, and with the support of Ron Dennis and the McLaren team, he was ready to take the next step toward a professional career that would take him to the top of Formula 1.

His career took a significant leap when he began competing in the British Formula Renault Winter Series in 2001, finishing fifth in the championship. From there, his progress was steady and full of successes, demonstrating that his talent in karting could translate into victories in single-seater categories. In 2002, Hamilton joined Manor Motorsport to compete in Formula Renault UK, where he finished fifth in the overall standings. His performance during that season secured him a seat for the following campaign with Manor, where he stood out by winning the championship, surpassing rivals like Alex Lloyd.

After securing the title, the Englishman skipped the last two races of the season to make his debut in the British Formula 3 Championship at its final round. However, his Formula 3 debut was unfortunate; in the first race, he suffered a puncture, and in the second, a collision with his teammate, Tor Graves, led him to the hospital. After surgery and rest, he fully recovered and returned to the track to finish the championship.

The following year, he competed in the full Formula 3 Euro Series championship with Manor Motorsport, where he finished fifth in the overall standings. He also won the prestigious Bahrain F3 Superprix and competed in the iconic Macau Formula 3 Grand Prix twice. The young British driver was on his way to proving his worth in the competitive world of Formula 3. During this period, Williams was close to signing Hamilton, but the lack of financial support from their engine supplier, BMW, led to the deal's collapse. However, Hamilton re-signed with McLaren, reaffirming his connection with the team that had believed in him since his karting days (Benson, n.d.).

In 2004, Hamilton had his first test with McLaren at the Silverstone Circuit. It was a crucial moment in his career, a sign that he was on the team's radar for future opportunities in Formula 1. That same year, he joined the ASM team to compete in the 2005 Formula 3 Euro Series, where he dominated the championship, winning 15 of the 20 rounds.

The next step for Hamilton was GP2, the category just below Formula 1. In 2006, he competed with ART Grand Prix, the sister team to ASM, and won the championship on his first attempt, beating rivals like Nelson Piquet Jr. and Alexandre Prémat. His performance in GP2 was outstanding; he achieved a dominant victory at Nürburgring despite receiving a penalty for speeding in the pit lane. At Silverstone, his home race, he executed an impressive move, overtaking two rivals at Becketts, a section of fast corners where overtaking is unusual. In Istanbul, he showed his ability to recover from setbacks, going from 18th place to second after an unexpected spin (Benson, n.d.).

Hamilton's GP2 victory coincided with a vacancy at McLaren after Juan Pablo Montoya left the team to join NASCAR and Kimi Räikkönen moved to Ferrari. The announcement of his promotion to McLaren for the 2007 season generated much speculation about who would be Fernando Alonso's teammate, the reigning world champion. After months of rumors, Hamilton was confirmed as the team's second driver, although the news wasn't made public immediately to avoid overshadowing Michael Schumacher's retirement announcement. The stage was set for Hamilton's much-anticipated Formula 1 debut, and the motorsport world eagerly awaited to see how this young talent would perform at the highest level of the sport.

Lewis Hamilton's debut in Formula 1 in 2007 was a transformative moment for the motorsport world. As the first Black driver to compete at the sport's highest level, his entry onto the track was a symbol of change and a wake-up call for an industry long marked by insularity, prejudice, and lack of diversity. For many young drivers from racial minorities worldwide, seeing Hamilton on the podium in his first race represented the promise of a future where talent and determination could overcome historical barriers of race and prejudice.

His first season with McLaren in 2007 was spectacular, partnering with two-time world champion Fernando Alonso. Hamilton made an immediate impact by reaching the podium in his debut and then winning his first Grand Prix in Canada, only on his sixth attempt. Throughout the season, he set several records, including the most consecutive podium finishes from debut (nine) and the most points in a debut season. Despite his success, his relationship with Alonso and the McLaren team became strained, culminating in Alonso's mutual contract termination in November. Hamilton finished as the runner-up in the 2007 World Drivers' Championship, losing the title to Kimi Räikkönen by just one point.

The following year, the Englishman achieved his first World Drivers' Championship in an exciting season finale (Benson, n.d.). Throughout 2008, he amassed five victories and ten podiums, including a memorable win at the British Grand Prix in the rain, one of the best performances in wet conditions in Formula 1 history. The season's climax came at the Brazilian Grand Prix, where Hamilton needed to finish at least in fifth place to win the championship. In a dramatic turn, he overtook Timo Glock in the final corners to secure the title, becoming the youngest champion at that time and the first British driver to win the championship since Damon Hill in 1996 (Eidell, 2024).

The following years at McLaren were marked by ups and downs. In 2009, the car was not competitive, and although Hamilton achieved some victories, the season was challenging. Despite this, Hamilton remained optimistic and worked hard to extract the best from the car. In 2010, he entered the final race with a chance to win the title but ended up fourth in the championship. In 2011, a season where personal distractions and clashes with the FIA affected his performance, he was surpassed by his teammate Jenson Button. However, he returned strongly in 2012, winning four races despite reliability issues and operational errors from the team. At the end of 2012, Hamilton announced his surprise departure from McLaren to join Mercedes in 2013, replacing the retiring Michael Schumacher.

Upon joining Mercedes in 2013, Hamilton reunited with his former karting teammate, Nico Rosberg. Although many considered his move to Mercedes a risk, the new turbo-hybrid engine era introduced in 2014 made the team a dominant force. Hamilton won his second world title in 2014 and continued his dominance in 2015, reaching the pinnacle of motorsport with his third world crown. His rivalry with Rosberg intensified, culminating in the 2015 United States Grand Prix, where Hamilton secured the title in an exciting wheel-to-wheel battle. The 2016 season was controversial, with Rosberg outdoing Hamilton by five points to win the title before retiring from the sport.

Starting in 2017, Hamilton faced an intense title battle with Sebastian Vettel from Ferrari. In 2017 and 2018, Hamilton demonstrated impressive consistency, surpassing Vettel to secure his fourth and fifth world titles. The 2019 season was another dominant year for Hamilton, securing his sixth championship at the United States Grand Prix and setting new records for points and podiums. The 2020 season, marked by the COVID-19 pandemic, saw Hamilton win his seventh world title, matching Schumacher's record, despite missing a race due to compliance with a coronavirus quarantine. This year marked the end of Hamilton's and Mercedes' dominance... for now.

That same year he was awarded the title "Sir" as part of the Queen's New Year's honors list, which recognized his exceptional achievements in Formula 1 and also his dedication to championing equality and social justice (Formula 1, 2020). For the seven-time world champion, being knighted was a testament to his impact beyond the racetrack. This title reflected how his success and his voice had inspired millions of people, demonstrating that greatness is measured not only in trophies and victories but also in a commitment to making the world a more just and equitable place. For the Black community and other underrepresented groups, the recognition was a symbol that change is possible and that barriers can be overcome, especially when perseverance and dedication are the guide. Sir Lewis Hamilton represents a role model, not only for those who aspire to be champions in motorsport but for all those who fight for a more inclusive and diverse future.

The following year, 2021 witnessed a fierce rivalry between Hamilton and the then-rookie Max Verstappen from Red Bull. The season culminated in a controversial Abu Dhabi Grand Prix, where Verstappen won his first title at the last moment after questionable decisions by the race director. Despite the controversy, Hamilton continued to demonstrate his skill and resilience, surpassing 100 wins and pole positions throughout the season.

In 2022, Mercedes faced technical difficulties with a problematic car, and Hamilton struggled to stay competitive. Despite these challenges, Hamilton achieved several podiums and set several race records, although he didn't win any races or secure a pole position for the first time in his Formula 1 career. During this season, Mercedes announced Hamilton's contract renewal until 2025, but before the start of the 2024 season, Hamilton decided to exercise an exit clause to leave the team at the end of 2024, seeking new challenges, as the 2024 season saw Mercedes failing to build a car worthy of a seven-time champion (Mercedes AMG F1, n.d.).

For 2025, Hamilton will join Ferrari, fulfilling a childhood dream. His arrival at Ferrari was received as one of the biggest surprises in Formula 1 history, marking the first time Hamilton would not drive a Mercedes-powered car. This change will end his record for most consecutive seasons with a single constructor, but it opens a new chapter in the career of one of the most successful drivers of all time (Meredith, 2024). With his perseverance and determination, Hamilton is ready to write a new chapter in Formula 1 history, this time with the iconic Ferrari team.

Impact and Advocacy

Sir Lewis Hamilton is a symbol of change and social commitment. Thanks to his work in the fight against racism, the promotion of diversity, the defense of human rights, and the protection of the environment and animals, as well as his extravagant taste in fashion, he has become an icon of activism and defending rights.

As the first and, to date, only Black driver to compete in Formula 1, Hamilton has faced unique challenges, including racism on and off the track. Throughout his career, he has been subject to racist abuse from fans and has often been treated unequally by the media and critics, often due to his ethnicity. Hamilton, however, has used these experiences as an engine to drive change. He has been vocal in the need for greater diversity in the sport, not only among drivers but also among teams and technical staff.

Hamilton has actively championed the ideals of inclusion and equity. In 2020, after the murder of George Floyd and the global protests that followed, Hamilton was a visible supporter of the Black Lives Matter movement, taking a knee before every race and wearing t-shirts with messages in support of the movement (Suhalka, 2022). He also criticized his colleagues and Formula 1 for their lack of reaction to systemic racism. Through the Hamilton Commission, a research group he founded to address the lack of diversity in motorsports, he has worked to identify the barriers that prevent Black people and other minorities from participating in the sport and has proposed concrete solutions to overcome them (Hamilton, 2010).

In 2021, he launched Mission 44, a foundation dedicated to empowering youth from underrepresented backgrounds to achieve their goals through education and employment. Hamilton has committed $25 million of his own wealth to support this cause. He has also collaborated with Mercedes to create Ignite, a joint initiative to increase diversity in motorsport, focusing on educational opportunities and financial support for those seeking careers in the sport.

Beyond his commitment to diversity and inclusion, Hamilton is also an advocate for sustainability and animal rights. Since 2017, Hamilton has followed a vegan diet, driven by concerns about animal welfare, the environment, and personal health. He has been outspoken about the environmental impact of the meat industry and has worked to reduce his own carbon footprint, selling his private jet and adopting electric vehicles (Powell, 2023). His veganism also translates into activism, supporting organizations that fight illegal wildlife trafficking and promoting sustainable alternatives in motorsport, such as the use of vegan materials in cars (Enjoli, 2022).

Hamilton uses his platform to advocate for these causes and his social media presence to spread positive messages about inclusion, social justice, and sustainability. He also invests in sustainable businesses and supports several charities, including UNICEF, Save the Children, and the Make-A-Wish Foundation. His commitment to positive change is a testament to how athletes can use his influence to make the world a better place (Powell, 2023; Enjoli, 2022). As a leader in sports and an activist for social causes, Hamilton has shown that it takes more than talent to be a true champion: it takes heart, courage, and a strong will to change the world for the better.

Legacy of Perseverance

Lewis Hamilton's legacy of perseverance is a reminder of the power of determination and compassion to change the world. Throughout his life, Hamilton has faced challenges that would have made many turn back, but instead, they shaped his character and forged his kind, humble, and compassionate personality. From his beginnings as a child in a working-class family in Stevenage to becoming a Formula 1 world champion, Hamilton's journey has been marked by relentless effort and a firm conviction that any obstacle can be overcome.

Hamilton grew up in an environment that didn't necessarily offer a clear path to success in motorsport. His family didn't have the typical resources of young race car drivers, and he often had to deal with racism and discrimination. From an early age, he was subjected to racial abuse, both at school and on karting tracks, and these experiences led him to learn to stand up for himself while also treating others with empathy and respect.

His journey to the top wasn't straightforward. Hamilton faced rejection, prejudice, and doubts about his ability to compete at the highest level. Despite these adversities, he persevered, staying focused on his dreams and working tirelessly to prove his worth. The sacrifice and commitment of his father, who worked several jobs to support his career, also motivated him to never give up, even when the odds seemed stacked against him.

The seven-time champion's attitude toward success has always been a mix of humility and confidence. Despite winning seven world championships and breaking numerous records, he never let fame change him. His willingness to work as a team and the way he celebrates his victories with his teammates reflect his gratitude for those who helped him get there. Moreover, his empathy and humility have led him to use his platform to advocate for important causes and to inspire others to believe in themselves, regardless of their backgrounds.

His legacy of perseverance is also evident in his activism and advocacy for diversity and inclusion. He knows that his position as the only Black driver in Formula 1 puts him in a unique role to drive change. By advocating for social justice and equal opportunities, Hamilton demonstrates that personal success can and should be used to create a positive impact on society.

His story teaches us that every challenge is an opportunity for growth and that the path to success may be difficult, but with perseverance and compassion, it is possible to reach great heights and make the world a better place. The way Hamilton has overcome adversity and chosen to use his position for the common good inspires us all to be kinder, more resilient, and committed to our own struggles and, ultimately, to leave a positive mark on our surroundings.

Chapter 7:

"Toto" Wolff—Strategy

In daily life, we all face challenges that require more than simple solutions. We need a strategic mindset to get ahead. Being a strategist means seeing the big picture, anticipating obstacles, and making bold decisions to achieve our goals. Strategy is an essential tool for managing complicated situations and turning problems into opportunities.

"Toto" Wolff, the current leader of the Mercedes-AMG Petronas team in Formula 1, is an excellent example of someone who has mastered the art of strategy. From managing people to making critical decisions in high-pressure moments, Wolff proves that strategy is the key to sustainable success. His skills offer valuable lessons for anyone who wants to approach life's challenges with a more calculated and effective approach.

Wolff's role as head of a Formula 1 team requires uniting people with different skills and experiences towards a common goal. His strategy is based on a deep understanding of human dynamics and the importance of keeping everyone motivated and focused. This type of strategic leadership is applicable to any setting, whether at work, at home, or in the community.

In this chapter, we will explore how "Toto" Wolff's strategic skills can teach us to be more effective in our daily lives. From making decisions under pressure to managing teams and balancing risks and rewards, his experiences in the world of Formula 1 will show us how a strategic approach can be the difference between success and failure.

If you've ever faced a challenge that seems insurmountable or wondered how to make the right decisions moving forward, this chapter will give you the tools and knowledge to approach your problems with a strategic mindset.

From Finance to Formula 1

Born on January 12, 1972, in Vienna, Austria, to a Polish mother and a Romanian father, Torger Christian Wolff, or "Toto" as his parents called him since he was a baby, had a childhood filled with challenges. His mother was a physician, and his father, who was a businessman, was diagnosed with brain cancer when Toto was only 8 years old. The illness led to his parents' separation and marked the beginning of difficult times for the young Wolff (Enzinger, 2011).

Toto Wolff began to demonstrate his strategic skill and determination from a young age. He attended the prestigious French school Lycee Français de Vienne, where he excelled academically and gained a broader perspective on life. Despite personal hardships, he remained focused and committed to his studies, laying the groundwork for his future career.

His first encounter with racing came at the age of 17 when he went to watch a friend compete at the Nürburgring circuit (Silbermann, 2016). The excitement and adrenaline of motorsport captured his attention, and he soon found himself racing in the Austrian Formula Ford Championship. Between 1992 and 1994, Wolff participated in several Formula Ford races in Austria and Germany, showcasing his skill and tenacity on the track. His most significant achievement during this period was winning his category in the 24 Hours of Nürburgring in 1994 (Fanamp, 2023).

However, Wolff had an eye for business and a pragmatic approach to life. He decided to focus on his business career, studying at the Vienna University of Economics and Business. In 1998, he founded his first investment company, Marchfifteen, followed by Marchsixteen. Although initially focused on investments in technology and internet companies, his approach expanded to strategic investments in industrial and publicly listed companies.

Despite his business success, Wolff's love for motorsport never waned. In 2002, this passion resurfaced, leading him to return to racing, this time as a co-owner of a driver management company alongside two-time Formula 1 World Champion Mika Häkkinen. Wolff found a way to merge his passion for racing and his business acumen in 2009 when he bought a stake in the

Williams Formula 1 Team. This investment was crucial, as it allowed him to enter the realm of Formula 1 from a leadership position.

In 2012, Wolff was appointed Executive Director of Williams. He led the team during a critical moment and contributed to their first victory in eight years at the Spanish Grand Prix. Toto Wolff's time at Williams helped him refine his leadership and strategic skills. During his tenure, he worked to improve efficiency and performance, giving him a clear perspective on how to manage a team in the highly competitive world of Formula 1. His strategic approach and ability to work with people were key to his later success with Mercedes.

In 2013, Wolff joined Mercedes-AMG Petronas Formula One Team as Executive Director and partner, acquiring a 30% stake in the team. This move marked the beginning of a golden era for Mercedes, where Wolff's strategic leadership was crucial in driving the team to a series of unprecedented successes.

One of his first successes was establishing the team as a dominant force in the hybrid engine era, which began in 2014. Under his leadership, Mercedes won the Constructors' and Drivers' Championships for seven consecutive years, a historic record in Formula 1.

His leadership was characterized by a combination of analytical rigor, people-management skills, and an innate ability to identify and develop talent. Wolff not only focused on maximizing the team's performance on the track but also on creating a workplace culture that promoted excellence and collaboration. One of his key philosophies was the "open-door leadership" approach, where team members felt valued and were encouraged to contribute innovative ideas.

Wolff also played a crucial role in developing drivers within the team. Under his direction, Mercedes signed Lewis Hamilton, who would go on to become one of the most successful drivers in Formula 1 history (Barstow, 2020). Hamilton's success, along with the team's consistency, demonstrated Wolff's focus on talent and sustained performance. His role as a strategist was essential in key decisions related to car development and race management.

Wolff stood out for his ability to adapt to changing conditions and adjust the team's strategy accordingly. A notable example was his handling of the W13 incident in 2022, a major challenge that led Mercedes to reconsider its technical and strategic approach. In addition to his success on the track, Wolff was also an advocate for diversity and inclusion in motorsport. He worked to expand opportunities for women in the sport and promoted initiatives to attract people from diverse backgrounds into the world of Formula 1.

In 2020, Wolff signed a new contract with Mercedes, extending his role as Executive Director and team leader until 2023 (Barstow, 2020). This agreement ensured his continuity and allowed Mercedes to maintain its momentum in a sport where change is constant.

The Fallout

We already know who this controversial figure in the world of motorsport is and where he comes from. Now, we can examine the repercussions of Toto Wolff's riskiest strategic decisions in his career. Let's start with his most famous gamble: the development and launch of the W13, the car that the Mercedes-AMG Petronas Formula One Team used for the 2022 season. During that time, the inherent risks of innovation and audacity in high-level competition were exposed, showing that even the most astute leaders can face unexpected challenges.

The W13 was the vehicle that the Mercedes-AMG Petronas Formula One Team unveiled for the 2022 Formula 1 season, a car designed to compete under the FIA's new technical regulations. These changes aimed to increase competition and improve overtaking capabilities on the track. Toto Wolff, as the team's leader and strategist, was responsible for guiding Mercedes through this transition, but the W13's design turned out to be a significant risk with unexpected consequences.

One of the most notable aspects of the W13 was its innovative design, which included a highly refined body structure and a unique floor concept. However, this bold approach soon revealed serious issues related to porpoising, a phenomenon that resulted in oscillating vibrations at high speeds due to the car's aerodynamics. This problem not only affected the vehicle's performance on the track but also caused discomfort for the drivers, especially Lewis Hamilton, who experienced back pain after the first races of the season (Daly, 2023).

Wolff, known for his ability to make strategic decisions under pressure, had to address the W13's problem with urgency. While other competing teams like Red Bull and Ferrari took advantage, Mercedes struggled to find solutions to the porpoising, which severely impacted their results in the early races of the season. Wolff had to restructure the team's priorities to mitigate the problem, which involved revising the vehicle's design and reevaluating the team's overall strategy.

This problem-solving process also impacted the team. Stress and pressure increased, and the dynamic within Mercedes, which had dominated Formula 1 for years, was tested. Wolff's decisions were critical in stabilizing the team and seeking solutions while also maintaining morale and fostering resilience during tough times (Hughes, 2023). As Mercedes attempted to correct its course, Red Bull took the opportunity to gain ground, marking the beginning of a new chapter in Formula 1.

The W13's problems not only affected Mercedes but also had repercussions across the broader Formula 1 landscape. The team's struggle to adapt to the new regulations allowed Red Bull and its star driver, Max Verstappen, to take the lead in the competition for the 2022 season title. This shift in the balance of power was a reminder of the volatile and competitive nature of Formula 1, where even the most successful teams can face significant setbacks.

The W13 challenge and Toto Wolff's response showed that leadership and strategy in Formula 1 require adaptability and creativity. The incident served as a clear example of how a calculated risk can have unpredictable consequences, impacting both the team's performance and the broader competitive landscape. However, it also highlighted Wolff's resilience and ability to lead Mercedes through challenging times by seeking innovative solutions to get back to the top.

The Two-Sided Nature of Strategy

The art of strategy is a complex and multifaceted discipline that often defines success in competitive environments like Formula 1. It involves a deep understanding of the current landscape, the ability to anticipate future trends, and the willingness to take risks that can lead to either triumph or failure. Toto Wolff embodies the essence of strategic thinking. His tenure at Mercedes has seen incredible success, but the case of the W13 demonstrates how even the most carefully planned strategies can sometimes lead to unexpected setbacks.

When Mercedes introduced the W13 for the 2022 season, the team took a bold step into uncharted territory. The new technical regulations presented an opportunity for innovation, and Mercedes aimed to continue its dominance with a revolutionary design. However, the car's issues with porpoising became a significant problem. This unforeseen challenge not only hampered the car's performance but also caused discomfort to the drivers, affecting the team's results.

The W13 situation serves as a stark reminder that strategy, no matter how well thought out, carries inherent risks. The failure of the W13 to meet expectations contributed to the end of Mercedes' dominant streak in Formula 1, paving the way for Red Bull Racing to rise to prominence. Toto Wolff's strategic gamble ultimately led to a two-year derailment for Mercedes, as the team worked to correct the issues and regain its competitive edge. This transition period highlighted the two-sided nature of strategy: the same bold decisions that can lead to success can also expose vulnerabilities.

Being a strategist means more than just devising plans—it requires the ability to adapt to changing circumstances and recover from setbacks. Wolff's response to the W13 incident demonstrated his resilience and his capacity to navigate turbulent times. While the immediate impact of the porpoising issue was significant, Wolff and his team worked tirelessly to find solutions, even as Red Bull surged ahead. This process of trial and error, learning from mistakes, and iterating on strategies is crucial for sustained success in any field.

The broader lesson from the W13 incident is that setbacks are an inevitable part of the strategic journey. No strategy is foolproof, and every decision carries the potential for failure. However, it's the response to failure that defines true strategists. Wolff's ability to lead Mercedes through challenging times, maintaining morale and fostering a culture of resilience, is a testament to his leadership and strategic acumen.

But nothing is said in the paddock, and it would be very unfair to reduce Wolff to his mistake with the W13 when his clear strategic ability meant no less than seven manufacturers' championships for the team.

In a sport as fiercely competitive as Formula 1, the margin for error is slim, and the consequences of a misstep can be severe. However, the willingness to take risks and the capacity to learn from failure are essential traits for success. The W13 incident underscores the importance of flexibility and adaptability in strategy. It serves as a reminder that even when things don't go as planned, the journey isn't over. There's always an opportunity to regroup, reassess, and come back stronger.

Ultimately, the two-sided nature of strategy is what makes it both challenging and rewarding. It's a constant balancing act between risk and reward, innovation and stability. The key is to remain open to new ideas, embrace the learning process, and never be afraid to make bold moves, even if they don't always work out. By understanding this duality, we can become better strategists in our own lives, prepared to face challenges and seize opportunities with courage and resilience.

Neither our greatest successes nor our greatest failures define us. Learning to accept challenges and take mistakes as a learning opportunity is a sign of courage, humility, and wisdom.

Chapter 8:

Carlos Sainz Junior—Loyalty

Loyalty is a quality that is cultivated through commitment, integrity, and dedication to the values and people we consider important in our lives. Relationships and alliances are often tested in life, and that is when loyalty is presented as a fundamental pillar that sustains and strengthens human bonds. This virtue is not only displayed in times of success and celebration but also, and perhaps more tellingly, in times of challenge and adversity.

Loyalty takes on a particular dimension in motorsport and, more specifically, in Formula 1. Here, drivers and teams operate under constant pressure, with each race and each season presenting new challenges and opportunities. In this competitive environment, loyalty is not simply an option—it is a necessity that can make the difference between success and failure, between team cohesion and chaos.

Carlos Sainz Jr. is a living example of this virtue. His career in Formula 1 is marked by a solid loyalty to his teams and colleagues, a characteristic that has earned him the respect and admiration of everyone in the paddock. From his beginnings in karting to his rise to the pinnacle of motorsport, Sainz has demonstrated a dedication and commitment that goes beyond what was expected.

Sainz's loyalty is manifested in his ability to remain true to his principles and to the people who have supported him throughout his career, even when circumstances are difficult. It is not easy to remain loyal when faced with tempting offers from rival teams or when the results are not as expected. However, Sainz has proven time and time again that his word and his commitment are sacred.

This loyalty not only strengthens his career but also has a profound effect on those around him. His teams know that they can count on him in the toughest moments, and that certainty creates an environment of trust and mutual respect. Sainz's loyalty fosters a spirit of collaboration and cohesion that is essential for success in a sport as competitive as Formula 1.

We can apply this lesson in various aspects of our lives. In our relationships, loyalty strengthens ties with family and friends, creating an environment of trust and mutual respect. In the professional field, being loyal to our colleagues and our organization can lead us to build more solid and cohesive teams, capable of overcoming any obstacle.

Despite difficulties and temptations, staying true to our values and the people who support us is a path to success and lasting respect.

The Heritage

In the home of a living legend like the two-time world rally champion, Carlos Sainz Sr., the passion for motorsport was passed down from generation to generation. Carlos Sainz Jr., born on September 1, 1994, inherited this passion but decided to swap dirt tracks for paved circuits. From a very young age, young Carlos showed a natural inclination toward motorsport. At 2 years old, his godfather, Juanjo Lacalle, gave him a battery-powered toy car, with which young Carlos demonstrated a surprising skill for drifting.

His father's influence was a constant in Sainz Jr.'s life. In 2004, when Carlos was 10 years old, he attended a tribute to his father for his retirement from the World Rally Championship with his family. This event marked a turning point in young Carlos' life, who began to dream of forging his own path in the world of motorsport (Motorsport, n.d.; López, 2014).

Sainz's journey in motorsport formally began in 2005, when he started karting at the age of 11. Although successes were not immediate, his perseverance and talent soon paid off. In 2006, he was crowned champion of the Madrid Championship, secured second place in the Race of Champions, and finished third in the Minikarts Industry Trophy (López, 2014). These initial achievements were just the beginning of a series of victories that would confirm his potential as a driver.

In 2007, Sainz continued accumulating triumphs and won the International City of Alcañiz Trophy. The following year, at 14, he won the Asia-Pacific KF3 Championship and was runner-up in the Spanish Championship in the same category. His skill and determination on the track did not go unnoticed, and in 2009, he won the prestigious Monaco Kart Cup, as well as achieving runner-up positions in both the European and Spanish KF3 Championships (Miquel, 2009).

These successes caught the attention of Red Bull, which invited Sainz to participate in tests for their young drivers' program. With support from Emilio and María de Villota, who helped him prepare for the test at the Jarama circuit, Sainz impressed the evaluators and joined the Red Bull Junior Team (Miquel, 2009). This opportunity was crucial for his professional development, giving him access to high-level resources and training.

The following year, at the age of 15, Sainz moved to Formula BMW Europe with the EuroInternational team. His performance was impressive, winning the Rookie Driver of the Year trophy and finishing fourth in the championship. Concurrently, he competed in the Formula BMW Asia-Pacific, where, although ineligible for points, he secured three victories, including a standout performance at the legendary Macau circuit.

The next step in his career came in 2011 when he competed in the full season of the Eurocup Formula Renault 2.0 with Koiranen Bros. Motorsport. Sainz finished second in the championship with 200 points, achieving two wins and ten podiums in fourteen races. Additionally, he participated in the Northern European Formula Renault 2.0 with the same team, where he was crowned champion three races before the end of the season, becoming the youngest driver to win the championship with ten victories and seventeen podiums.

In 2012, Sainz debuted in the F3 Euroseries as a guest driver with the Signature team for the final round in Hockenheim, securing a fifth place and two retirements. The following year, he returned to the F3 Euroseries, where he finished ninth in the championship with just two podiums. He also competed in the British Formula 3 Championship, finishing sixth, and in the European Formula 3 Championship, where with six podiums, he achieved fifth overall. Additionally, he participated in prestigious events such as the Masters of Formula 3 and the Macau Grand Prix.

In 2013, Sainz signed with MW Arden for a season in the GP3 Series. Although he faced some challenges, he achieved two podiums and finished tenth in the championship. He also participated in select events of the Formula Renault 3.5 Series with Zeta Corse, which led to his signing by DAMS for the following season. In 2014, Sainz dominated the Formula Renault 3.5 Series, achieving seven victories and being crowned champion with a significant lead over his competitors (El Mundo, 2014).

The culmination of his efforts came in 2015 when Scuderia Toro Rosso announced that Sainz would be an official driver for the Formula 1 season, alongside Dutchman Max Verstappen. In his first year, Sainz broke the Spanish debut record by qualifying higher than any other Spanish driver up to that point. Despite several retirements due to mechanical issues, Sainz showcased his ability and potential, scoring points in several races and finishing the season in fifteenth place with 18 points.

In 2016, Sainz improved on his initial performance, scoring points in nine of the first eleven races and finishing tenth in the championship. However, the second half of the season presented challenges due to a decline in the car's performance. Nevertheless, Sainz finished the season twelfth with 46 points, an improvement from the previous year.

Finally, in 2017, Sainz continued to prove his worth at Toro Rosso before being signed by Renault for the final races of the championship. His best result of the year was a fourth place in the Singapore Grand Prix, solidifying his reputation as a talented and resilient driver.

After a notable performance with Toro Rosso, Sainz moved to Renault to replace Jolyon Palmer from the United States Grand Prix onwards. In his debut, Sainz achieved seventh place and finished the season in ninth place in the championship. In 2018, Sainz faced a challenging year at Renault, finishing tenth in the championship, behind his teammate Nico Hulkenberg. His best result was fifth place in the Azerbaijan Grand Prix.

The switch to McLaren in 2019 marked a turning point. Sainz became a team leader, outperforming several midfield drivers and securing his first podium in the Brazilian Grand Prix, starting from the last position. This achievement made him the second driver in F1 history to reach a podium from the last grid position. He finished the season in sixth place, demonstrating an outstanding adaptation to the team and solidifying himself as a strong competitor on the grid.

In 2020, Sainz continued with McLaren, showing consistency and resilience. Despite initial problems and several retirements due to bad luck, like the puncture in Britain and issues in Belgium, he stood out with a second place in Monza and several impressive comebacks, such as in the races in Turkey and Bahrain. His performance significantly contributed to McLaren finishing third in the Constructors' Championship, the team's best position since 2012. That year was also marked by the announcement of his signing with Ferrari for the 2021 and 2022 seasons (Infobae, 2020).

At Ferrari, Sainz continued to showcase his talent and adaptability. In 2021, he debuted with Ferrari, achieving several podiums, including second place in Monaco and third place in

Hungary, Russia, and Abu Dhabi, finishing fifth in the Drivers' Championship, outperforming his teammate Charles Leclerc. In 2022, Ferrari showed a significant performance improvement, and Sainz achieved his first Formula 1 victory at the British Grand Prix, along with several pole positions and podiums. He finished the season in fifth place in the Drivers' Championship, consolidating his reputation as one of the best drivers on the grid.

The 2023 season was one of mixed challenges and successes for Sainz. He scored points regularly, with his best result being a third place in Monza and an impressive victory in Singapore, where he demonstrated excellent strategy and driving under pressure. However, he faced difficulties such as the collision in Australia and the retirement in Belgium. The season concluded with Sainz in seventh place in the Drivers' Championship and Ferrari losing second place in the Constructors' Championship to Mercedes.

In 2024, the pre-season brought significant changes with the announcement of Lewis Hamilton's addition to Ferrari for the 2025 season, replacing Sainz. The season started promisingly for Sainz, securing a podium in Bahrain before undergoing appendicitis surgery and missing the race in Saudi Arabia. However, he returned to Australia, achieving a victory after Verstappen's retirement, and continued with good results, including a third place in Japan (Motorsport, 2024). These achievements underscore his ability to overcome adversity and his crucial role in Ferrari's strategy and success on the tracks.

Legacy of Loyalty

As we have seen, Carlos Sainz Jr.'s childhood and adolescence were always linked to motorsport. Carlos Sainz, his father, was going through the twilight of his rallying career in 2006, 14 years after winning his last world title when his son was racing karts in Madrid for the first time. Carlos Sainz Jr. was 12 years old. Despite his father's absence due to his commitments in the rally championship, young Carlos never resented him. On the contrary, he understood that his father was pursuing his dreams, just as he would one day, showing a deep loyalty to his father and mentor.

Carlos Sainz Sr. acknowledged the difficulty of being absent from his son's races. "Many times I couldn't be at his races because I was in the rally championship," said Sainz Sr. in an interview: "For both of us, it was difficult because other parents were with their children. However, racing has always been a bond for us" (Arenas, 2018). This mutual understanding and support forged a strong bond between them, based on a shared passion for racing.

Carlos Sainz Jr. faced additional challenges beyond his father's absence. As the son of a motorsport legend, he felt immense pressure to prove himself on his own merits. In an interview with the Spanish broadcaster Onda Cero Radio (2024), Sainz Jr. revealed that other drivers were eager to beat him because of his illustrious surname. "I couldn't let them beat me; I wanted to prove that I was there because of my talent and not just because of my surname," he said. This determination and self-imposed pressure to excel reflects his loyalty to his ambitions and his father's legacy.

From these experiences, we can extract several lessons about loyalty that apply to our lives. First, understanding and supporting the dreams of our loved ones, even when it involves enduring physical distance or personal sacrifices, can strengthen our bonds. Carlos Jr.'s acceptance of his father's absence, knowing it was due to the pursuit of his dreams, highlights the importance of empathy and support in relationships. This perspective can help us maintain strong connections, even when our paths temporarily diverge due to professional or personal goals.

Secondly, remaining true to our own aspirations while honoring our heritage is a powerful form of loyalty. Carlos Jr.'s determination to prove himself on the track, despite the shadow of his father's legacy, teaches us the value of perseverance and self-confidence. By striving to achieve our goals with integrity and dedication, we can build our legacy while respecting the influences that have shaped us.

Furthermore, Carlos Sainz Jr.'s ascent to Formula 1 with Toro Rosso, Red Bull's subsidiary, marked a milestone in his career and was a crucial moment that demonstrated his loyalty to his team and his determination to overcome obstacles. Despite being teammates with Max Verstappen, a young prodigy who quickly gained favoritism from engineers, Carlos did not allow this to undermine his confidence or his commitment to the team. Rather, he used this situation as an opportunity to push himself further and constantly improve.

The agreement with Red Bull allowed Carlos the possibility of advancing to a higher level each year, provided he demonstrated good performance on the track and successfully completed his academic studies, which he alternated with his racing career. Despite the dual demands of his life, he never had academic problems, highlighting his discipline and focus both in the classroom and on the track. His persistence and skills earned him a title in the Formula Renault 3.5 in 2014, which opened the doors to a seat at Toro Rosso in Formula 1.

The camaraderie between Carlos Sainz Jr. and Max Verstappen was a highlight of their time together at Toro Rosso. Despite internal competition and pressure from the team, Carlos greatly valued Verstappen and his skill as a driver. Despite natural preferences toward Max Verstappen by many engineers, Carlos did not allow this to discourage him; instead, he used it as motivation to strive even harder and constantly improve.

When Verstappen was promoted to Red Bull halfway through the 2016 season, thus closing the possibilities of a promotion for Carlos within the team, he showed no resentment or disillusionment. Instead, he accepted the challenge with determination and remained committed to his career, accepting the opportunity to be loaned to Renault for the 2018 Formula 1 season.

Carlos Sainz Jr.'s commitment and loyalty to his team and his career are inspiring examples of how to face competition and adversity with determination and professionalism. Instead of resenting the team's decisions or his teammates, Carlos chose to seize every opportunity to improve and prove his worth on the track. His ability to stay focused on his goals and keep moving forward even in challenging circumstances is a valuable lesson that we can apply in our own lives to strengthen our relationships and achieve our dreams.

The 2024 season was a period of challenges and learning for Carlos Sainz Jr. at Ferrari. Despite facing the news that his contract would not be renewed for the following season, Carlos demonstrated unwavering loyalty to his team and his teammates. Although it might have been tempting to become discouraged or disengage from the team in this situation, Carlos chose to maintain his commitment and professionalism until the last moment.

During the development of the season, which has six races at the time I am writing these lines, Carlos is showing exceptional dedication both on and off the track. His hard work, work ethic, and ability to overcome obstacles are evident in every race. Despite the difficulties and the uncertainty about his future with the team, Carlos remains focused on giving his best and supporting Ferrari in its quest for positive results.

His loyalty to Ferrari and his teammate and friend Charles Leclerc is a touching testament to his character and professionalism.

Ultimately, the story of Carlos Sainz Jr. reminds us of the importance of loyalty, determination, and perseverance in pursuing our dreams. Through his experiences, we learn that true loyalty goes beyond external circumstances; it is a deep commitment to our values, our teammates, and our goals. May Carlos's story inspire us to face challenges with courage, to stay true to ourselves, and to never lose sight of our dreams, even in the toughest times.

Chapter 9:

Max Verstappen—Discipline

Discipline is one of the most admirable and necessary qualities to achieve success in any area of life. It is about the ability to maintain focus and consistency at work, keep going even when circumstances are adverse, and set and meet long-term goals. Discipline is cultivated through repetition and commitment to oneself.

It is the force that drives us to get up early to train, to study when we would prefer to rest, and to keep going when the results do not come as quickly as we expect. Without discipline, goals become distant dreams and promises to ourselves remain mere unfulfilled intentions.

Max Verstappen is a living example of how discipline can transform talent into sustained success. From a young age, Max demonstrated an innate ability for motorsports, but it was his discipline that led him to become one of the most outstanding drivers in Formula 1. Throughout his career, we have witnessed how his dedication, focus, and unwavering commitment have led him to overcome obstacles, continually improve, and maintain an exceptional level of performance.

Max was born into a family deeply linked to motorsports. His father, Jos Verstappen, was also a Formula 1 driver, and from a very young age, Max was surrounded by the culture and rigor of the sport. This environment not only provided him with the necessary opportunities to develop his talents but also instilled in him a work ethic and a disciplined mindset from an early age. Known for his tenacity and experience, Jos made sure Max understood that talent would only take him so far—the rest would depend on his effort and discipline.

From his early years in karting, Max showed an unusual commitment for his age. While other children could easily become distracted or lose interest, Max stayed focused on improving every aspect of his performance. He spent hours training, perfecting his technique, and learning about the technical aspects of the vehicles he drove. This early dedication not only allowed him to excel in the junior ranks but also laid the foundation for his success at higher levels.

Max's discipline is not limited to his physical training. On the court, he is known for his ability to remain calm under pressure and make quick, accurate split-second decisions. This ability to maintain focus and control in high-tension situations is a testament to his mental discipline, something he has developed over years of experience and training.

However, discipline is not simply a matter of physical and mental training. It is also reflected in Max's lifestyle. From his diet to his training regimen to his dedication to the simulator, every aspect of his life is geared toward improving his performance on the track. Max understands that to be the best, he cannot afford to neglect any detail, and this meticulousness is a clear example of his discipline.

In a race as competitive and demanding as Formula 1, discipline can be the difference between success and failure. Max Verstappen shows us that, with a disciplined mindset, it is possible to achieve and maintain a high level of performance, overcoming challenges and achieving goals that others can only dream of. Max's journey shows us that with discipline and dedication, we can achieve great things and make our most ambitious dreams come true.

The Making of a Disciplined Driver

Max Emilian Verstappen was born on September 30, 1997, in Hasselt, Belgium, and he grew up in the Belgian city of Maaseik, near the border with the Netherlands. In fact, that's where he attended school and other activities. He grew up in a family deeply involved in motorsport. His father, Jos Verstappen, was a Formula 1 driver from 1994 to 2003, and his mother, Sophie Kumpen, also competed in go-karts at a professional level. From birth, Max was surrounded by an environment where motorsport was not only a passion but a way of life. This early influence would be fundamental in shaping his character and developing his career (Red Bull Racing, 2018).

From a very young age, little Max showed exceptional talent for driving. At the age of 4, he was already driving a go-kart that his parents rented for him, and his innate ability soon became evident. However, this talent did not develop spontaneously— it was nurtured through a rigorous training regimen imposed by his father. His father, Jos Verstappen, known for his strong character and high expectations, spared no effort to ensure that his son had every possible opportunity to excel in motorsport, but this also involved strict and sometimes controversial discipline.

Max's childhood was marked by a delicate balance between unconditional support and severe demands. Jos not only trained Max in driving techniques but also mentally prepared him for the pressures of the sport. The training sessions were intense and meticulous, and Jos insisted on perfection in every aspect of Max's performance. This rigorous approach was not without tensions. There were times when the pressure and expectations from Jos were overwhelming for a young Max. However, these experiences also forged a resilient mindset and an unquestionable work ethic in the young driver.

As Max grew, his dedication and discipline began to bear fruit. His success in karting competitions was notable, and he soon became a well-known name in youth motorsport circles. He won numerous championships: his initial success was in the Belgian Mini Class championship, where he won all 21 races in 2006, demonstrating his natural ability and impressive capacity to stay focused and consistent under pressure. This period was crucial for his development, as it established the foundations of the work ethic and discipline that would be defining characteristics of his career (Driver Database, n.d.).

His rise in karting was unstoppable. In 2007, he dominated the Rotax Mini Max Klasse, winning all 18 races. He continued his dominance in 2008 and ventured into more competitive championships, such as the Benelux Rotax Mini Max Klasse, where he won 11 of the 12 races. These achievements allowed him to quickly move up to the Cadet Class in the Belgian championship, where he again won the title with eleven victories in twelve races. In 2009, he joined the Pex Racing team and won the Belgian Minimax and KF5 championships, cementing his reputation as one of the brightest prospects in karting (Driver Database, n.d.).

In 2010, Verstappen made the leap to international karting, competing in world and European championships with the CRG team. In the KF3 World Cup, he finished second behind Alex Albon but took revenge by winning the WSK Euro Series and the WSK World Series, beating drivers like Robert Vişoiu. His success continued in 2011 and 2012 when he won the WSK Euro Series and the WSK Master Series in the KF2 class. In 2013, at the age of 15, he won the KF and KZ European championships and became the KZ World Champion in Varennes-sur-Allier, France, the highest category in karting (Driver Database, n.d.).

His talent did not go unnoticed, and in 2014, Verstappen ventured into single-seater racing, participating in the Florida Winter Series and debuting in the European Formula 3 with Van Amersfoort Racing. His impressive performance, which included ten victories and a third-place finish in the championship, caught the attention of Red Bull. At the end of 2014, he joined the Red Bull Junior Team and, at 17 years old, became the youngest driver to participate in a Formula 1 weekend during the free practice sessions of the Japanese Grand Prix (Richards, 2014).

The leap to Formula 1 came in 2015 when Max was signed by Toro Rosso, becoming the youngest driver to compete in the top category of motorsport. His debut was a historic moment, and his performance in his rookie season exceeded expectations. Max displayed a maturity and skill that belied his youth, quickly earning the respect of his peers and the public.

Max's discipline and focus were reflected primarily in his preparation off the track. He maintained a strict routine of physical and mental training, understanding that success in Formula 1 requires more than just talent. His dedication to continually improving, analyzing every detail of his performance, and working closely with his team were key factors in his rapid rise.

In 2016, Max made the switch to Red Bull Racing, a move that marked a turning point in his career. His first race with Red Bull was the Spanish Grand Prix, and Max was not only impressed with his performance but won the race, becoming the youngest driver to win a Formula 1 Grand Prix. This achievement was a testament to his ability, but also to his discipline and his capacity to handle pressure in crucial moments.

Throughout his career at Red Bull, Max has continued to demonstrate his exceptional ability to compete at the highest level. His disciplined approach is reflected in his consistency on the track, his ability to make quick strategic decisions, and his capacity to remain calm under pressure. Max has won numerous races and shown a remarkable ability to learn and adapt, continually improving his performance (Benson, 2022).

The 2021 season was a decisive year for Max as he won his first Formula 1 World Championship. This achievement was not only a testament to his talent and skill but also to his discipline and dedication. Throughout the season, Max showed impressive consistency, handling the pressure of competing against experienced drivers and teams with significant resources. His disciplined approach and ability to stay focused on his goals were key factors in his success.

Max's relationship with his team at Red Bull has also been an example of discipline and professionalism. The Dutchman has worked closely with his engineers and mechanics, demonstrating a deep understanding of the technical aspects of his car and an unwavering commitment to continuous improvement. His ability to communicate effectively with his team and his willingness to take responsibility for his own performance have been crucial factors in his success. So much so that he signed a contract extension with Red Bull until 2028, reflecting mutual trust and his long-term commitment to the team (Benson, 2022).

His absolute and unquestionable dominance in the 2022 and 2023 seasons secured his second and third-world titles with impressive performance. His sporting achievements are a testament to his exceptional talent and dedication to motorsport, cementing him as one of the standout drivers of his generation.

Off the track, it is known that the—for now—triple world champion maintains a disciplined lifestyle that reflects his commitment to his career. He is dedicated to a rigorous regimen of physical and mental training, ensuring he is in the best possible shape to compete.

Max has also shown remarkable maturity in his approach to victories and defeats. Despite the ups and downs of his career, he has maintained a positive attitude and a focus on learning and improvement. Max Verstappen's story is an inspiring example of how discipline can transform talent into success. From his early days in karting to his rise to the top of Formula 1, Max has demonstrated a dedication and focus that distinguishes him as one of the standout drivers of his generation. His relationship with his father, which we will delve into next, has been a constant source of motivation and discipline, and his ability to handle pressure and stay focused on his goals is an example for all of us.

Legacy of Discipline

Max Verstappen's legacy of discipline is a complex blend of rigor, determination, and controversy, offering both inspiring and cautionary lessons on how discipline can shape success and character. His relationship with his father, Jos Verstappen, is one of the most influential and discussed aspects of his upbringing.

From a very young age, Max was subjected to an extremely strict training regime imposed by his father, who was a Formula 1 driver with very high expectations for his son. Jos was known for his tough demeanor and relentless pursuit of perfection, often using methods that crossed the line into what many would consider toxic discipline. A notable example of this occurred when, after a poor performance in a karting race, Jos abandoned Max at a gas station, leaving him there as punishment. Additionally, there are reports of aggressive behavior from Jos toward mechanics and team staff, reflecting an attitude that prioritized success at any cost (Culliford, 2021).

This extreme approach raises important reflections on how discipline can become harmful. While rigidity and high expectations can push someone to exceed their limits, they can also create an environment of fear and resentment. The obsession with perfection and intolerance of frustration can have detrimental effects on mental and emotional health, both for the one imposing the discipline and the one receiving it. It is crucial to balance discipline with emotional support and understanding to prevent it from becoming a source of trauma.

The story of Max and Jos Verstappen underscores the need to build disciplined habits from a perspective of mental well-being, where the drive for excellence does not sacrifice personal health and happiness.

In contrast, the current champion's routine and focus in his Formula 1 career demonstrate how discipline can be applied in a healthy and effective manner. Despite admitting that he hates exercising (Christensen, 2023), Max maintains a strict and personalized training routine that caters to his specific needs as a driver. He prefers working out at home, mainly using his body weight and resistance bands. This approach allows him to stay in shape without the need for complex equipment or heavy weights, making it more manageable and less tedious.

Max has also expressed his preference for listening to his body rather than relying on devices like smartwatches to monitor his performance. This practice highlights the importance of developing an intuitive connection with one's own body, which is essential for maintaining a balance between physical discipline and mental well-being. His training focus is not on achieving extreme physical form but on optimizing his condition for the specific demands of his sport. This involves a combination of cardio and strength exercises, always intending to enhance his performance on the track (Ilic, 2021; JOE, 2022).

Max's diet also reflects adaptive and mindful discipline. He maintains a healthy and controlled diet to ensure he is in the best possible shape to compete, but he also allows himself small indulgences to relax. This flexibility is crucial to avoid mental and physical burnout, demonstrating that effective discipline does not mean constant restriction but a sustainable balance between effort and relaxation.

Another key aspect of Max's preparation is adapting to the extreme conditions of Formula 1, such as the high temperatures and humidity during races. The strength required to handle a Formula 1 car, especially in the legs for braking, and the ability to withstand significant loss of body mass during a race, require a rigorous training regimen and dietary discipline. Max and his Red Bull Racing team work meticulously to optimize every aspect of his performance, which has led to his dominance in recent seasons (JOE, 2022).

In the story of the Dutchman, we find the motivation and inspiration needed to tackle our own most cherished goals. His example shows us that for those who do not fear sacrifice, no bet is too high. As you advance in your goals, remember that effective discipline is the one that propels you forward without sacrificing your well-being. Find your balance, listen to your body and mind, and let the passion for what you do guide your path to success. Max shows us that with the right combination of rigor and self-care, there are no limits to what you can achieve.

Book Review Request

I hope you've enjoyed diving into the epic stories of the nine motorsports legends we shared. What did you think of those captivating narratives? Did they inspire you to overcome your challenges with more determination and passion?

I would love to know your opinion on this. Would you take a moment to leave me your impressions in the form of a review? Your feedback is essential to continuing to improve and offer you inspiring content that reaches thousands of people and changes their lives.

Thank you for being part of this incredible adventure.

Epilogue

As we close this book, we cannot allow the teachings of these legends to simply remain within the printed pages. They are shining beacons in the darkness, guiding us on our journey to greatness. They remind us that life is a marathon, not a sprint toward a fleeting goal and that the true prize lies in the path we tread and the people we become along the way.

So, I challenge you, dear reader, to take these virtues, these life lessons, and make them your own. May Fangio's resilience inspire you to rise every time you fall, stronger and more determined than before. May Senna's determination burn in your heart, propelling you to pursue your dreams with an unrelenting passion that knows no bounds or barriers.

May McLaren's vision take you beyond the confines of the known, challenging you to explore new frontiers and discover new horizons. May Schumacher's leadership guide you in your endeavors, reminding you that the true leader is not the one at the forefront, but the one who serves others.

May Alonso's humility keep you grounded, reminding you that true power lies in the ability to learn, grow, and adapt. May Hamilton's perseverance give you the strength to keep moving forward even when the odds are against you, and may Wolff's strategy help you chart your own course to success with cunning and foresight.

May Carlos Sainz Jr.'s loyalty inspire you to uphold your commitments and values, reminding you that true greatness lies in fidelity to your principles and unwavering support for those around you.

And finally, may Verstappen's discipline remind you that the path to greatness is neither easy nor comfortable but that every step forward, every sacrifice made with determination, and every challenge overcome with discipline brings you one step closer to your boldest dreams.

Do not remain motionless, waiting for greatness to find you. Step onto the track of life with determination and courage and make every day count. Commit yourself to applying these virtues in every aspect of your life, to surpass yourself each day, and to never give up on your dreams, no matter how daunting they may seem.

Because at the end of the day, what truly matters is not the trophies you accumulate or the achievements you reach, but the person you become along the way. And on that journey to greatness, may these lessons and virtues be your compass, your guide, and your constant inspiration.

Life is a race, dear reader, and you are the driver of your destiny. So, grip the wheel tightly, accelerate toward your dreams, and never look back. The world is waiting for your greatness—what are you waiting for?

References

A Tribute to Life Network. (2011, December 9). *San Marino Grand Prix – Imola 1994*. https://www.ayrton-senna.net/san-marino-grand-prix-imola-1994/

A Tribute to Life Network. (2018, February 2). *Martin Brundle on great Ayrton Senna*. https://www.ayrton-senna.net/martin-brundle-on-great-ayrton-senna/

Allen, J. (2000). *Michael Schumacher*. Bantam Books.

Arenas, A. (2018, March 22). *Carlos Sainz Jr., infancia y destino en el automovilismo*. El Financiero. https://www.elfinanciero.com.mx/deportes/carlos-sainz-jr-infancia-y-destino-en-el-automovilismo/

Autosport. (2000, June 29). *"Senna was the greatest ever" - Schumacher*. https://www.autosport.com/f1/news/senna-was-the-greatest-ever-schumacher-5028448/5028448/

Barstow, O. (2020, December 18). *Toto Wolff, Ineos to take equal stake in Mercedes F1, Wolff stays as team boss*. Crash. https://www.crash.net/f1/news/950438/1/toto-wolff-ineos-take-equal-stake-mercedes-f1-wolff-stays-team-boss

Bautista, J. (2020, May 10). *Fernando Alonso y su ídolo de la infancia: "Era contradictorio, ni quería pilotar en esa categoría."* La Sexta. https://www.lasexta.com/noticias/deportes/motor/fo

rmula1/fernando-alonso-idolo-infancia-era-
contradictorio-queria-pilotar-esa-
categoria_202005105eb7cfe44f7187000162b7d9.html

Benson, A. (n.d.). *Challenger, champion, change-maker.* BBC Sport.
https://www.bbc.co.uk/sport/extra/c1nx5lutpg/The-
real-Lewis-Hamilton-story

Benson, A. (2022, March 3). *Verstappen signs new Red Bull contract.*
BBC Sport.
https://www.bbc.co.uk/sport/formula1/60599389

Christensen, M., & Téllez, A. (2023, August 22). *El entrenamiento
de Max Verstappen para ganar en la F1.* GQ.
https://www.gq.com.mx/articulo/max-verstappen-
rutina-de-entrenamiento-y-dieta

Christensen, M. (2022, August 8). *Lewis Hamilton: The F1
superstar on controversies, racism, and his future.* Vanity Fair.
https://www.vanityfair.com/style/2022/08/cover-
story-lewis-hamilton-never-quits

Christensen, M. (2023, August 21). *Max Verstappen has an
approach to working out that is all of us.* British GQ.
https://www.gq-magazine.co.uk/article/max-
verstappen-workout-diet-fitness

Coleman, M. (2023, August 17). *F1's "Crashgate" scandal returns as
Felipe Massa seeks justice for a lost title.* The Athletic.
https://theathletic.com/4785380/2023/08/17/f1-
crashgate-felipe-massa-nelson-piquet-jr/

Collings, T. (2005). *Team Schumacher.* Highdown.

Culliford, G. (2021, December 13). *Inside Max Verstappen's relationship with dad once arrested for attempted murder*. The US Sun. https://www.the-sun.com/sport/4265896/inside-max-verstappens-relationship-with-dad-jos/

Dagless, G. (2023, July 18). *Ayrton Senna v Alain Prost: F1's greatest rivals*. GiveMeSport. https://www.givemesport.com/ayrton-senna-alain-prost-f1-mclaren/

Daly, C. (2023, February 19). *What went wrong for Mercedes during the 2022 season and their W14 car*. Mail Online. https://www.dailymail.co.uk/sport/formulaone/article-11760437/What-went-wrong-Mercedes-2022-season-2023-W14-Formula-1-car.html

de Menezes, J. (2014, April 30). *F1 legend Senna in his own words 20 years after his death*. The Independent. https://www.independent.co.uk/sport/motor-racing/ayrton-senna-senna-in-his-own-words-as-world-remembers-the-20th-anniversary-of-his-fatal-crash-9205960.html

Donaldson, G. (n.d.). *Michael Schumacher*. Formula 1® - the Official F1® Website. https://www.formula1.com/en/drivers/hall-of-fame/Michael_Schumacher.html

Donaldson, G. (2019). *Ayrton Senna*. Formula 1® - the Official F1® Website. https://www.formula1.com/en/drivers/hall-of-fame/Ayrton_Senna.html

Driver Database. (n.d.). *Driver: Max Verstappen.*
https://www.driverdb.com/drivers/max-verstappen

Economic Times. (2024, January 9). Michael Schumacher
health update: F1 icon able to sit at dinner table with
family. Will he recover? *The Economic Times.*
https://economictimes.indiatimes.com/news/internati
onal/us/michael-schumacher-health-update-f1-icon-
able-to-sit-at-dinner-table-with-family-will-he-
recover/articleshow/106686140.cms?from=mdr

Eidell, L. (2024, February 25). *All About Lewis Hamilton's Parents,
Anthony Hamilton, and Carmen Larbalestier.* People
Magazine. https://people.com/all-about-lewis-
hamilton-parents-8598016

El Mundo. (2014, October 18). *Carlos Sainz júnior se proclama
campeón de las World Series.*
https://www.elmundo.es/deportes/2014/10/18/5442
89bdca47412f748b4577.html

Enjoli, A. (2022, January 7). *Lewis Hamilton on human rights, clean
cars, and his love of animals.* LIVEKINDLY.
https://www.livekindly.com/lewis-hamilton-animal-
rights/

Enzinger, G. (2011, March 14). *Der Toto-Gewinner» Wolff,
Williams, Formel, Toto, Zeit, Zeiten» WIENER.*
Web.archive.org.
https://web.archive.org/web/20110314083140/http:/
/www.wienerpost.at/2010/11/der-toto-gewinner/

Fanamp. (2023, October 8). *Toto Wolff: A deep dive into his life and legacy in Formula 1.* https://www.fanamp.com/pe/toto-wolff

Formula 1. (n.d.). *Fernando Alonso.* https://www.formula1.com/en/drivers/fernando-alonso

Formula 1. (2020). *Arise, Sir Lewis! Hamilton to be awarded knighthood after historic seventh world title.* https://www.formula1.com/en/latest/article/arise-sir-lewis-hamilton-to-be-awarded-knighthood-after-historic-seventh.2oKynH8fOmJytSk8mOo0o9

Formula 1. (2023, December 22). *Schumacher's key lesson learned from Hamilton and Russell.* https://www.formula1.com/en/latest/article/schumacher-reveals-the-key-lesson-learned-from-hamilton-and-russell-after.7EpmSorXaBXWeDnEhB1NJr

Fry, N. (2019). *Survive. Drive. Win.* Atlantic Books.

Haldenby, N. (2016, April 28). *Imola 1994: The full story.* Lights Out Blog. https://www.lightsoutblog.com/imola-1994-the-full-story/

Hamilton, L. (2010). *Lewis Hamilton: My story.* HarperCollins UK.

Henry, A. (1998). *Wheel to wheel.* Phoenix.

Hilton, C. (2007). *Michael Schumacher: The whole story.* Haynes Publishing.

Hindle, S. (2024, March 18). *How Bruce McLaren's death shaped more than just his F1 team*. Motorsport. https://www.motorsport.com/f1/news/how-bruce-mclaren-death-shaped-more-than-just-his-f1-team/10588701/

History of the McLaren. (n.d.). McLaren. https://www.mclarenphl.com/dealership/history.htm#:~:text=Founded%20by%20Bruce%20McLaren%20in

Hughes, M. (2023, May 17). *Why Mercedes has got F1's current era so wrong so far*. The Race. https://www.the-race.com/formula-1/why-mercedes-has-got-f1s-current-era-so-wrong-so-far/

Ilic, N. (2021, September 23). *How Max Verstappen trains his neck to prepare for the intense g-force on track*. Men's Health Magazine Australia. https://menshealth.com.au/how-max-verstappen-trains-his-neck-to-prepare-for-the-intense-g-force-on-track/?category=fitness

Infobae. (2020, May 14). *Oficial: Carlos Sainz es el nuevo piloto de Ferrari*. Infobae. https://www.infobae.com/america/deportes/2020/05/14/oficial-carlos-sainz-es-el-nuevo-piloto-de-ferrari/

JOE. (2022, December 12). *Max Verstappen workout: "We don't do many weights"* [Video]. YouTube. https://www.youtube.com/watch?v=7BZFE5oRsqs&ab_channel=JOE

Juan Manuel Fangio, la gloria en cuatro ruedas. (2023, November 26). Hoy. https://diariohoy.net/interes-general/juan-manuel-fangio-la-gloria-en-cuatro-ruedas-245405

Lifona, D. G. (2016, September 7). *Fórmula 1: Fernando Alonso: "El último año en Ferrari me culpaban de todo."* Marca. https://www.marca.com/motor/formula1/2016/09/0 7/57cfebe4468aeb877e8b46cc.html

López, L. (2014, November 28). *Carlos Sainz Júnior: De tal palo, tal astilla.* Sport. https://www.sport.es/es/noticias/motor/formula1/ca rlos-sainz-junior-palo-astilla-3729424

Lyons, P. (n.d.). *Bruce McLaren.* Motorsports Hall of Fame of America. https://www.mshf.com/hall-of-fame/inductees/bruce-mclaren.html

Marchi, F. (2023, September 7). Genís Marcó, clave en el crecimiento de Alonso: "El primer día que lo vi pilotar..." Mundo Deportivo. https://www.mundodeportivo.com/motor/f1/202309 07/1002064725/genis-marco-clave-crecimiento-alonso-primer-dia-vi-me-sorprendio.html

Martin, J. (2023, May 1). *Ayrton senna y alain prost: La historia de un desengaño que es leyenda de la fórmula 1.* DAZN. https://www.dazn.com/es-ES/news/motor/ayrton-senna-y-alain-prost-la-historia-de-un-desengano-que-es-leyenda-de-la-formula-1/1vv7bdxtr913ozvdlittb8jmg

McLaren Cars. (n.d.). *Innovation.* Mc Laren. https://cars.mclaren.com/en/about/Innovation

McLaren Racing. (n.d.). *Bruce McLaren.* https://www.mclaren.com/racing/heritage/bruce-mclaren/

Mercedes AMG F1. (n.d.). *Lewis Hamilton - Driver.* https://www.mercedesamgf1.com/drivers/driver/lewis -hamilton

Meredith, S. (2024, February 1). *Formula 1 star Lewis Hamilton to leave Mercedes for Ferrari after 2024 season.* https://www.cnbc.com/2024/02/01/formula-1-star-lewis-hamilton-to-join-ferrari-media-reports-say.html

Miquel, C. (2009, October 6). *Carlos Sainz Jr. piloto Red Bull por cinco años.* Diario AS. https://as.com/motor/2009/10/06/mas_motor/1254 844219_850215.html

Motorsport. (1995, May 8). *Juan Manuel Fangio died at 84.* https://au.motorsport.com/f1/news/juan-manuel-fangio-dead-at-84/1660429/

Motorsport. (n.d.). *Carlos Sainz perfil - biografías, noticias fotos y videos.* https://es.motorsport.com/driver/carlos-sainz/37111/

Museo Juan Manuel Fangio. (n.d.). *El Comienzo De La Historia.* Museo Fangio. https://www.museofangio.com/es/juan-manuel-fangio/biografia/4-cuarta-parte-1950-1958/

Onda Cero Radio. (2024, April 20). *Sainz cree que la maniobra "optimista" de Alonso terminó costándole el sprint a ambos.* Onda Cero. https://www.ondacero.es/deportes/motor/sainz-cree-que-maniobra-optimista-alonso-termino-costandole-sprint-ambos_2024042066236479c0b95c0001081434.html

Oporto, E. (2015, October 5). *Las dos carreras "perdidas" de Alonso*. Marca. https://www.marca.com/2015/10/05/motor/formula1/1444072828.html

Powell, N. (2023, October 30). *Sir Lewis Hamilton: The road to diversity*. Last Word on Motorsports. https://lastwordonsports.com/motorsports/2023/10/30/sir-lewis-hamilton-the-road-to-diversity/

Red Bull Racing. (2018). *Max Verstappen: Driver profile*. Red Bull. https://www.redbull.com/es-es/athlete/max-verstappen

Richards, G. (2014, October 3). Max Verstappen becomes the youngest man to drive a Formula One car. *The Guardian*. https://www.theguardian.com/sport/2014/oct/03/max-verstappen-becomes-youngest-man-to-drive-a-formula-one-car

Senna. (2023, October 10). *Carrer on the tracks*. Senna. https://senna.com/en/journey-senna/career-on-the-tracks/

Silbermann, E. (2016, September 4). *Breakfast with ... Toto Wolff*. F1i. https://f1i.com/magazine/69794-breakfast-toto-wolff.html

Suhalka, M. (2022, June 28). *How F1 goat Sir Lewis Hamilton is breaking the barriers of racing with phenomenal initiative*. Essentially Sports. https://www.essentiallysports.com/f1-news-how-f1-

goat-sir-lewis-hamilton-is-breaking-the-barriers-of-racing-with-phenomenal-initiative/

The World Economic Forum. (2022, December 2). *How companies can support people with disabilities at work*. World Economic Forum. https://www.weforum.org/agenda/2022/12/4-ways-businesses-can-support-employees-with-disabilities/

TN Deportivo. (2022, July 17). *A 27 años de la muerte de Juan Manuel Fangio, cómo fueron sus cinco títulos*. Todo Noticias. https://tn.com.ar/deportes/automovilismo/2022/07/17/a-27-anos-de-la-muerte-de-juan-manuel-fangio-como-fueron-sus-cinco-titulos/

Traducciones, L. (2021, April 29). *Ayrton Senna: Karting years*. Ayrton Senna. https://www.ayrton-senna.net/ayrton-senna-karting-years/

V., J. (2009, September 3). *Alonso: "Tuve una infancia muy feliz."* Sport. https://www.sport.es/es/noticias/motor/formula1/alonso-tuve-infancia-feliz-809640

Watson, F. (2021, September 14). *Inside Schumacher and Senna feud as German left "upset" by fellow F1 legend*. The Mirror. https://www.mirror.co.uk/sport/formula-1/michael-schumacher-ayrton-senna-netflix-24981121

Woodhouse, J. (2022, April 16). *Ferrari's Mattia Binotto learned how to be a leader from Michael Schumacher*. PlanetF1. https://www.planetf1.com/news/michael-schumacher-taught-mattia-binotto-leadership